LITTLE
LESSONS FROM THE
MYSTICS

Other Books by Bob Burnham

Little Lessons from the Saints

LITTLE
LESSONS FROM THE
MYSTICS

52 SIMPLE AND SURPRISING
WAYS TO EXPERIENCE THE
MYSTERIES OF FAITH

BOB BURNHAM

LOYOLAPRESS.
A JESUIT MINISTRY
Chicago

LOYOLAPRESS.
A JESUIT MINISTRY

3441 N. Ashland Avenue
Chicago, Illinois 60657
(800) 621-1008
www.loyolapress.com

Scripture quotations are from *New Revised Standard Version Bible: Catholic Edition*, copyright © 1989, 1993 National Council of the Churches of Christ in the United States of America. Used by permission. All rights reserved worldwide.

Cover art credit: cristinabagiuiani/iStock/Thinkstock, Shutterstock

ISBN: 978-0-8294-4924-2
Library of Congress Control Number: 2020947506

Printed in the United States of America.
20 21 22 23 24 25 26 27 28 29 Versa 10 9 8 7 6 5 4 3 2 1

If the doors of perception were cleansed everything would appear to man as it is, infinite.

For man has closed himself up, till he sees all things through narrow chinks of his cavern.

—William Blake

Contents

Mᴙsᴛɪᴄs ᴏɴ Mʏ Mɪɴᴅ xi

Hᴏᴡ ᴛᴏ Usᴇ Tʜɪs Bᴏᴏᴋ xiii

Part One The Incarnation 1

  1 Scripture: Origen of Alexandria 3

  2 Contemplation and Action: Martha and Mary 7

  3 Mirroring: Clare of Assisi 11

  4 Hazelnuts: Lady Julian 15

  5 Body: Teresa of Ávila 19

  6 Serenity: Mary of Jesus of Ágreda 23

  7 Nearness: Karl Rahner 27

  8 Intimacy: Bernard of Clairvaux 31

  9 Motherhood: The Blessed Virgin Mary 35

10 Humility: Thomas à Kempis 39

11 Apophasis: Dionysius the Areopagite 43

12 Interconnection: Pierre Teilhard de Chardin 47

13 Convergence: Ilia Delio 51

Part Two The Paschal Mystery 55

14 Suffering: Paul of the Cross 57

15 Bridging: Catherine of Siena 61

16 Discontent: Hadewijch of Antwerp 65

17 Grief: Margery Kempe 69

18 Hope: Maria Esperanza Bianchi 73

19 Heartfulness: Clare of Montefalco 77

20 Disappointment: Francis of Assisi 81

21 Affliction: Rita of Cascia...85
22 Tragedy: Marguerite Porete 89
23 The True Self: Thomas Merton 93
24 Darkness: John of the Cross 97
25 Continuity: Catherine of Genoa.................................101

Part Three The People of God 105

26 Covenant: Abraham 107
27 Pacifism: John Paul II...111
28 Irrationality: Marie de l'Incarnacion 115
29 Righteousness: Elizabeth of Töss 119
30 Service: John the Evangelist.......................................123
31 Liturgy: Hildegarde of Bingen 127
32 Reality: Thomas Aquinas..131
33 Harmony: Paul the Apostle 135
34 Forgiveness: Helen Prejean 139
35 Justice: Moses..143
36 Reconciliation: Jacob..147
37 Kinship: Nicholas Black Elk.......................................151
38 Interspirituality: Wayne Teasdale.............................155

Part Four The Most Holy Trinity 159

39 Pathways: Elisabeth of Schönau................................161
40 Milestones: Gertrude the Great 165
41 Epiphany: Anne Catherine Emmerich..................169
42 Silence: Henri Nouwen..173
43 Morality: Amma Syncletica 177
44 Joy: Bridget of Sweden 181
45 Attention: Peter of Alcántara....................................185

46 Presence: Brother Lawrence of the Resurrection.................. 189

47 Inscape: Gerard Manley Hopkins........................... 193

48 Detachment: Meister Eckhart................................. 197

49 Divine Love: Mechthild of Magdeburg 201

50 Paradox: Richard Rohr............................. 205

51 Forgetfulness: An Anonymous Mystic 209

52 Awareness: Ronald Rolheiser.................................... 213

EPILOGUE: IGNATIUS OF LOYOLA 217

ACKNOWLEDGMENTS 219

ABOUT THE AUTHOR.. 221

Mystics on My Mind

In this book, I share little lessons from mystics.

Mysticism is often defined as union with the divine. Mystics, I always thought, had supernatural experiences like ecstatic dreams and visions or spiritual markings like the stigmata, or could defy the laws of physics by levitating or bi-locating. Maybe that's the reason I was attracted to mysticism in the first place. I mean, seriously, who wouldn't want superpowers? Look out, Spider-Man. Now these aren't lessons about how to *be* a mystic. Nor are they lessons that try to explain an understanding of some of the greatest questions our faith poses: How is Jesus true God and true human? Why did Jesus have to die? What did Jesus mean when he told us to love one another? How is God three and one at the same time? The truth is, I can't help you answer those questions because I'm not sure of them myself.

After spending time getting to know the stories of different mystics, I know now that **mysticism is about recognizing that our ordinary experiences are supernatural because**

God is present in them. We just have to learn how to recognize God's presence. That's what I hope to accomplish with this book: I hope the lessons I share here will help you find God in all things, in places you would expect him to be, in places you'd never think of looking, and in places where you were sure God couldn't be.

We need to learn how to do this now more than ever. We face major challenges as a species. Our planet is crying out to us for help, and we cannot hear her because we cannot find God in our sister Mother Earth. We are infatuated by violence because we are unable to find God in our sisters and brothers. We chase after comfort and happiness because we cannot find God in ourselves.

We cannot find God because we have spent our time looking for answers to our deepest questions. Instead, we need to learn to be comfortable with mystery. By *mystery*, I mean these basic questions: *Who is God?* and *Who am I?* They are the heart of the mystic, that is, someone who lives the mysteries, who lives with these questions because every answer is, at best, inadequate or always evolving.

How to Use This Book

I offer lessons from fifty-two people whose writings, stories, and examples have helped me find God in all things. Each of them presents a specific mystery that helps me live one of the four biggest mysteries of my Catholic faith: the Mystery of the Incarnation (the Second Person of the Holy Trinity became human), the Paschal Mystery (the suffering, death, resurrection, and ascension of Jesus Christ), the Mystery of the People of God (Jesus Christ is present in his Church), and the Mystery of the Most Holy Trinity (The Three Persons of the Trinity: God the Father, God the Son, and God the Holy Spirit are One).

I begin each lesson with a brief summary of what I learned from a mystic. These are not detailed biographies or summaries of mystical teachings. Rather, I share with you how that mystic impacted me and my faith and how I live the Christian life. What I offer is my own wisdom, not theirs. I make no claim of authority. I readily admit that I do not fully grasp what these mystics taught in the entirety of their lives. I invite you to investigate these mystics more closely on your own. In fact, I hope that you become lifelong friends with the people in this book and learn from them yourselves.

Following this summary is a short practice to help you find God in all things. This section begins with a short Scripture verse for you to ponder, followed by something you can do to live—that is, to be aware of—the following mysteries in your daily life:

- **The Incarnation.** To encounter the Mystery of the Incarnation is to see that Christ is the model for all created things. We can find God because, in becoming human, God found us.

- **The Paschal Mystery.** This mystery helps us understand that even though suffering is not something we seek, it is part of the process of holiness. Through the Paschal Mystery, we can find God in and through our suffering.

- **The People of God.** The mysteries of Christ teach us how to live as part of a community. We are the People of God—a living, breathing body. This mystery reveals the fact that we find God in our relationships.

- **The Trinity.** This is the mystery of God's very self. To live this mystery is to enter into the flow of love between the Three Persons of the Trinity. We find God when we love others.

You may recognize some of the mystics I included in this book. You will meet St. Teresa of Ávila (who teaches me that I can find God in my body) and St. John of the Cross (who points out that using my imagination to find God has its limits). You'll encounter great mystics like Mechtild of Magdeburg (who shows me that falling in love is the surest path to finding God), Hildegarde of Bingen (who reminds me to find God in my rituals), and the great Dominican thinker, Meister Eckhart (who focuses on the necessity of detachment). You'll also meet people you may have never heard of, like Margery Kempe (who found God despite her many temptations) or Marguerite Porete (whose mysticism got her burned at the stake). There are also people you might not expect, people who don't fit the mold of a mystic: there are biblical figures like Abraham, Jacob, and Moses and modern thinkers like Karl Rahner, Richard Rohr, and Ilia Delio. You'll even meet people like Helen Prejean, the anti-death-penalty activist (who herself might be surprised that she's even mentioned here).

I included these people for a simple reason: each, in their own way, has showed me how to find God, and I hope they will help and inspire you in your faith journey. Some of these people are saints, meaning that they have been canonized by the Catholic Church. But many aren't. That doesn't make them any less holy, nor does it mean that their lessons aren't as valuable. You don't have to be canonized a saint to be a mystic—all you have to do is seek God.

I wrote this book with the intention that you would spend a week with each mystic. Since there are fifty-two mystics in this book, you can spend an entire year finding God in all aspects of your daily life. But you don't have to use this book that way. You can use it as a way to deepen your prayer life during a liturgical season such as Advent (the mystics of the Incarnation are good for that) or Lent (the mystics of the Paschal Mystery would be great Lenten companions). You may simply want to use this book as an introduction to certain mystics or to learn a new practice to incorporate into your daily prayer.

Simply put, there is no right or wrong way to use this book. Use it in any way that helps you grow closer to God. Let the Holy Spirit be your guide.

A Blessing

I hope this book helps you see the mysteries not as abstract theological propositions but as ways to find God everywhere. I hope it will help you grow in love, mercy, and compassion. I hope it helps you learn how to make friends with the phrase *I don't know, and I don't need to know; I want to love.*

So, as you begin this journey with the mystics, let me offer you the following blessing:

May the Lord bless you and keep you.
May the Lord shine his face upon you and be gracious to you.
May the Lord look kindly upon you and give you peace.

Part One

The Incarnation

The Mystery of the Incarnation is that the Second Person of the Most Holy Trinity, the Son, took on human flesh in the person of Jesus Christ without loss of his divinity. In other words, God came to live as one of us, to experience everything we did—the good, the bad, and the ugly. Perhaps this mystery is what makes finding God in all things even possible: we can find God in the here and now because God chose and (continues to choose) to dwell among us.

The mystics I present in this part have helped me understand that God continues to abide with us. They have helped me realize that "finding God in all things" simply means that God is present in the incarnate reality of the world. And I sincerely hope their stories will inspire you as they did me and that the practices will serve to help you find God in the world around us.

1

Scripture

Origen of Alexandria

c. 184–c. 253

The Scriptures were written by the Spirit of God, and have a meaning, not such only as is apparent at first sight, but also another, which escapes the notice of most. For those (words) which are written are the forms of certain mysteries and the images of divine things.

—Origen of Alexandria

The Big Bang theory is a cosmological model that explains how the universe began. About fourteen billion years ago, the universe—matter, energy, and time—formed a cosmic singularity. That singularity went through a period of rapid expansion: within 10^{-35} seconds (that's way faster than you can imagine), it increased its size by a factor of 10^{50} (that's way bigger than you can imagine). It was kind of like an explosion—hence the Big Bang.

Scripture gives us another cosmological model (well, two actually). According to those models, God created the universe and everything in it within a few days. Young Earth Creationists take this biblical account literally. According to their calculations, the universe is only six to ten thousand years old.

I am not a Young Earth Creationist. I do not read the Bible literally. That does not make me a heretic. Rather, I follow the advice of Origen of Alexandria, one of the Fathers of the early Church. Parts of Scripture are not to be understood in a literal sense—or to use his word, in a "historical" sense—because Scripture is meant to be understood spiritually. Scripture reveals "mystical economies" that cannot be understood by the literal meaning of words alone. Origen is someone we need to listen to. He was an intellectual giant whose lectures and writings influenced the development of Christian theology.

Origen's "mystical economy" asks us to look at the body, soul, and spirit of Scripture. "For as man is said to consist of body, soul, and spirit," writes Origen in his work *On the First Principles*, "so also does sacred Scripture."

The *body* of sacred Scripture is the literal meaning of the words themselves. These words provide our initial understanding of Scripture. However, Origen explains that "it was the design of the Holy Spirit . . . to show that we were not to be edified by the letter alone." The *spirit* of Scripture is the search for the allegorical meaning of the words. It's the meaning *behind* the meaning, which can be searched by one's intellect. The *soul* of Scripture is the hidden meaning of the text that arises when the reader is detached from the literal or allegorical meaning. If the body is the meaning of the words themselves, and the spirit is the meaning behind the words, then the soul is the meaning of the Word without words.

Scripture is not like any other text. It reveals a hidden meaning—divine mysteries—where we can find God, and human language is incapable of that task.

Awareness and Practice

And the Word became flesh and lived among us, and we have seen his glory, the glory as of a father's only son, full of grace and truth.

—John 1:14

To live the Mystery of the Incarnation, we must live the Mystery of Scripture. Just as the Son of God became human in every way but sin, God's Word—which existed before time—was expressed using human language. You can live the mystery by engaging with the body, spirit, and soul of Scripture.

Read a short passage from Scripture, such as a reading from the Mass of the day or any passage of your choice. First, approach the *body* of the text. What is being said? Who is the intended audience? What do the words mean in the context they were written? A good commentary can help you understand the body of the text.

Then approach the *spirit* of the text. Meditate on what you read: What is the allegorical meaning of the words? (Again, a commentary can be helpful.) How does the text apply to you today?

Finally, approach the *soul* of the text. Let go of any and all words. Simply rest in the silence of the text and listen closely. How is the meaning revealed without words?

2

Contemplation and Action

Martha and Mary

First Century

*But Martha was distracted by her many tasks; so she came to him
and asked, "Lord, do you not care that my sister has left me to do
all the work by myself? Tell her then to help me." But the Lord
answered her, "Martha, Martha, you are worried and distracted by
many things; there is need of only one thing. Mary has chosen the
better part, which will not be taken away from her."*

—Luke 10:40–42

Words matter. Maybe we give them too much weight—words
can be blunt instruments that are often imprecise. (Perhaps
that's why Jesus used images in his parables to describe the
kingdom of God; words alone just can't capture it.) But
regardless, we use words to reveal our mental and emotional
states. That's why psychologists use word-association tests.

These tests are simple enough. The psychologist offers a
word, and the subject responds with the first word that comes
to mind. The theory is that the word the subject comes up
with will reveal an emotional burden.

I'm not a psychologist, but I like games. So let's play a word-association game. Write down the *first* response that comes to your mind for each of the following words: *action, contemplation, Martha, Mary.* (You may want to write these words and your responses in your journal.)

In case you were interested, the words that came to my mind were *action/set; contemplation/rest; Martha/hedge; Mary/rose.*

The words that I chose to use for that game—*action, contemplation, Martha, Mary*—are important when talking about finding God in all things. The story of Martha and Mary is often used to describe the relationship between contemplation and action. Mary is the contemplative one: she rested at the Lord's feet (which would have been scandalous in Jesus' time: only disciples sat at a master's feet, and disciples were never women). Martha, in contrast, was complaining about doing what needed to be done to entertain a guest.

We know whom Jesus approved, and it wasn't Martha.

The problem with Martha was not that she was busy. The problem was that she was distracted. Unlike Mary, Martha's attention was directed away from the Lord. She was too attached to her feelings of annoyance toward her sister for not helping.

Perhaps that's why it's so hard for us to find God in anything today. Like Martha, we are distracted by many things. We can't focus on the Divine because we are too focused on accomplishing this task or achieving that goal. Not that our tasks and our goals are unimportant. The fact is, we need Marthas. We need people who can get stuff done.

To find God in all things, I have to learn how to keep my attention focused on the Lord while I do the stuff that needs doing. The trick is not to be Mary instead of Martha; the trick is to be Mary *while* being Martha.

Awareness and Practice

"Everyone then who hears these words of mine and acts on them will be like a wise man who built his house on rock. The rain fell, the floods came, and the winds blew and beat on that house, but it did not fall, because it had been founded on rock."

—Matthew 7:24–25

Participating in the presence of God means participating in the presence of others, and participating in the presence of others means participating in the presence of God. And isn't that exactly what the Incarnation accomplished? Through it, we see how God participates directly in humanity, and how humanity participates in the divine.

Unite your contemplation to action. As you practice the presence of God, how do you respond? What do you feel called to do? What fruits sprout from your contemplation? How do you share these fruits with others?

Unite your actions to your contemplation. As you go about your daily tasks, pay attention and ask yourself, *Where is God in this?* Wait for an answer. You may have to ask the question several times. If no answers seem to come, ask, *Where is God in this absence?*

3

Mirroring

Clare of Assisi

1194–1253

Place your mind before the mirror of eternity!
Place your soul in the brilliance of glory!
Place your heart in the figure of the divine substance
and, through contemplation, transform your entire being into
the image
of the Godhead Itself,
—Clare of Assisi

The 2017 Nobel Prize for physics was awarded to Rainer Weiss, Barry Barish, and Kip Thorne "for decisive contributions to the LIGO detector and the observation of gravitational waves." The LIGO (short for Laser Interferometer Gravitational-Wave Observatory) used lasers and mirrors to detect the presence of gravitational waves, which were first predicted by Albert Einstein in 1916.

But the LIGO's mirrors weren't ordinary mirrors—they were made from pure-fused silica glass, ground in Germany, and sent all around the world to receive more than eighty special coatings. As a result, these mirrors were nearly perfect:

they could reflect most of the laser light. (These mirrors were 99.999 percent reflective of the laser light, to be specific, yet they were translucent to the human eye!)

St. Clare of Assisi used mirrors too; in fact, mirrors are a major theme in her mysticism. Unlike the pure-fused silica glass found in the LIGO detectors, however, the mirror Clare used was 100 percent perfect: her mirror was Christ.

"Gaze upon that mirror each day . . .," Clare counseled Agnes of Prague, "that you may adorn yourself completely . . . with the flowers and garments of all the virtues." Her instruction to Agnes is meant for us as well: we are called to reflect on what we see by gazing on Christ and putting on the virtues of poverty, humility, and charity, just as Clare did.

Clare recalled how Christ came into the world naked and poor. Reflecting that image, Clare imitated Christ's poverty, humility, and charity. Clare herself became a mirror for others: "For the Lord Himself has placed us as a model, as an example and mirror not only for others, but also for our sisters whom the Lord has called to our way of life as well, that they in turn might be a mirror and example to those living in the world."

When we look at ourselves in the mirror of Christ, we too will be transformed into a reflection of God and become mirrors for others. And we find God in that mirror.

Awareness and Practice

For she is a reflection of eternal light,
a spotless mirror of the working of God,
and an image of his goodness.

—Wisdom 7:26

The Mystery of the Incarnation is the mirror of Christ: Christ perfectly reflects the Divine in the world. We, too, are mirrors, but we are imperfect ones. Sometimes we reflect the glory of God; other times, we reflect something much less noble.

Who, or what, reflects God in the world? What do these things reveal about what's in your heart? For example, if you see God in a beautiful sunset, where do you see your own beauty? If you see God in the generous spirit of another person, what do you see in your own generosity?

Similarly, who, or what, doesn't reflect God? What do these things reveal about what's in your heart? For example, if you see God's absence in the violence that plagues the world, what violence lurks in your heart? If you see God's absence in the selfishness of others, where in your heart does selfishness hide?

4

Hazelnuts

Lady Julian

c. 1342–c. 1416

I saw that He is to us everything that is good and comfortable for us: He is our clothing that for love wrappeth us, claspeth us, and all encloseth us for tender love, that He may never leave us; being to us all-thing that is good, as to mine understanding.

—Julian of Norwich

Julian of Norwich is a mystery.

All we know about her is that she withdrew from the world, enclosing herself in a small room at St. Julian's Church in Norwich, England. We don't even know her real name—she is only referred to by the name of the church where she lived. What little we do know of her comes from the book *Revelations of Divine Love*, the first book known to have been written by a woman in the English language.

Revelations of Divine Love is a classic in Christian spirituality. Anyone seeking to enter into the mystery of God can benefit from the "showings" she received from God during an illness that almost took her life. In one of these showings, God showed her a little secret, no more than the size of a hazelnut.

What may this be? Julian thought.

God answered: "It is all that is made."

The secret wasn't in the thing itself but in its properties: (1) God made it; (2) because God made it, God loves it; and (3) because God loves it, God keeps it. If something exists, Julian realized, it exists simply because God loves it. God is the Maker, the Keeper, and the Lover.

In this showing, Julian also recognized the secret to finding God in all things: we do not find God in the thing itself; we find God in the love with which God loves that thing.

I think I can find comfort in the right ideas. I might try to find rest in knowing that I belong to the right group. And I like to think I can relax by enjoying the fruits of God's creation. Yet, I can only find true comfort and rest in the realization that God loves me because God made me and God keeps me. And that truth about me is also true about all things. Whatever comfort I experience comes from God, and God alone, and not from ideas, groups, or possessions.

We find God in all things only when we realize how much God loves *everything*. And when we realize that God loves everything—including us—we can make Lady Julian's prayer our own: *Lord, give me yourself, for you are enough to me.*

Awareness and Practice

For God so loved the world that he gave his only Son, so that everyone who believes in him may not perish but may have eternal life. Indeed, God did not send the Son into the world to condemn the world, but in order that the world might be saved through him.

—John 3:16–17

The Mystery of the Incarnation teaches us that God loves what God made, which is everything. And God loves everything passionately! To fully encounter this mystery, we need to see that God loved not only the Son but also all creation. Perhaps that is how we are saved by God's Son: he shows us that God's love can be contemplated everywhere and in everything.

Take a moment and bring to mind two people: someone you love and someone who is a source of pain, sadness, or fear. Now, bring to mind two objects: one that is precious to you as well as one that you think is useless. Repeat the following phrase for several minutes: "They are all loved by God." Does your perception of these people and things change? Knowing that all these things are loved by God, do you see yourself as equally beloved?

Body

Teresa of Ávila

1515–1582

For this body of ours has one fault: the more you indulge it, the more things it discovers to be essential to it. It is extraordinary how it likes being indulged; and, if there is any reasonable pretext for indulgence, however little necessity for it there may be, the poor soul is taken in and prevented from making progress. Think how many poor people there must be who are ill and have no one to complain to, for poverty and self-indulgence make bad company.

—Teresa of Ávila

The human body is an amazing and mysterious place. Mary Roach, the author of the book *Gulp*, offers a fascinating perspective:

We were basically a tube, with a little bit around it. At a certain point, to get to food sources elsewhere, you needed some way to get around, so you start developing limbs or some mobility-type device, you need a brain to kind of coordinate things, and the gut had a primitive nervous system. It really is kind of the most elemental chunk of the human.

Consumption, it seems, is fundamental to what we as human beings do. The problem is that as human beings, if we don't regulate our consumption—if we do not moderate our appetites—we can become self-indulgent.

And self-indulgence, warns St. Teresa of Ávila, is a major obstacle for those seeking God.

Self-indulgence is a misguided effort to satisfy our deepest desires and cope with difficulties. The more we indulge, the more we become incapable of resisting temptation; instead, we believe that satiating our temptations is our just reward. We become consumed with feeling good because when we feel good about ourselves, we think that we can keep suffering—our own and that of others—at bay. When we are self-indulgent, we no longer seek God; we seek only to satisfy our appetites.

St. Teresa recommends that we guard against self-indulgent behavior by practicing self-mortification. As a result, inflicting pain on one's body was seen in centuries past as a virtuous discipline that helped people control their appetites and resist temptation. Self-mortification was even believed to be a way to unite oneself to the suffering of Christ.

Today we know better ways to combat self-indulgence. In fact, I'm sure that if St. Teresa knew what we know now about human psychology, I doubt she would recommend self-mortification at all. (She did, by the way, counsel moderation in subjecting oneself to mortification.) Instead, I think she would tell us to take care of ourselves, that we tend to our emotional, psychological, and spiritual well-being. We can eat healthy. We can exercise. We can get enough sleep.

Practicing self-care allows us to find God in the most obvious of places: our own body, which is a wondrous, beautiful miracle. This will require more than a little bit of moderation, which in our society can be a painful enough mortification.

Awareness and Practice

But God has so arranged the body, giving the greater honor to the inferior member, that there may be no dissension within the body, but the members may have the same care for one another.

—1 Corinthians 12:24–25

The Mystery of the Incarnation reaffirms that the human body is good—God the Son chose the human form to be God's dwelling place on earth! We *can* love our bodies, because God does. Self-denial, when seen from the perspective of love, teaches you to give your body only that which it needs to thrive.

You can live the Mystery of the Incarnation by maintaining a physically active lifestyle. By developing balance, flexibility, and strength, you will give your body what it needs to thrive. Witness your body praising God through the harmony of movement and the beautiful efficiency of the human organism.

Harvard Medical School identified the five best exercises you can do: swimming, tai chi, strength training, walking, and Kegel exercises. Before trying any of these, please consult your physician and a certified personal trainer to learn how to exercise safely and properly.

6

Serenity

Mary of Jesus of Ágreda

1602–1665

While Lucifer with his infernal legions in visible forms persisted in his unhappy attempts, the most serene Mary never looked upon them nor paid any attention to them, although by the permission of God She heard the uproar.

—Mary of Jesus of Ágreda

Whenever I feel I'm being tormented by demons, I rely on four simple words: *Shut the hell up*.

Now most of the time, I use the word *demons* to refer to ideas, thoughts, and feelings that torment me. One common demon is named Regret. Another one might be named Shame. Yet another might be named Unworthiness. Truly, such demons are legion.

I also think that demons are external, personal creatures. They are angels who reject God, and they want us to join in their rebellion. (However, sometimes I wonder if demons seek us out not as allies in their war but as weapons for it.) Demons can use mystical experiences as a recruiting tool.

It's a good strategy if you think about it. Demons might offer "heavenly" visions that are nothing but illusions meant to lead us astray. They might also offer visions that horrify us. Sometimes, after having a moment of mystical ecstasy, a demon might come around and fill us with incredible despair; the withdrawal is too painful to endure. Whatever their strategies, the demons have a singular goal: to deter us from living the mysteries by making the mystical path seem too dangerous. Instead of finding God in anything, we see demons everywhere. That's no way to live.

So, how can I try to find God without running into those demons? I don't think I can—it's an inherently dangerous search (which might explain why so many people are afraid to even try it, thus giving demons their victory without even a fight). But what I *can* do is learn a lesson from Mary of Jesus of Ágreda, a Spanish abbess best known for her six-volume book, *The Mystical City of God.* In this book, the Blessed Virgin Mary dictated her biography to Mary of Jesus.

Mary of Jesus chronicles the Blessed Virgin's struggles with the devil and his demons. The Blessed Mother's response was not to fight fire with fire, nor was it to avoid the mystical path altogether. Rather, as Mary of Jesus records, the Virgin Mary's response was always the same: she ignored them, commanded them to "stop their blasphemies," and sang praises to God.

"No strange or improper emotion could disturb the serenity of her heavenly interior," wrote Mary of Jesus.

In the face of torments—whether they're disturbing thoughts or a fallen angel—the best response is to remain calm and at peace, to recognize your wholeness in the eyes of God.

Awareness and Practice

"And do not bring us to the time of trial,
but rescue us from the evil one."

—Matthew 6:13

Jesus Christ was subjected to all types of torments in his human life—like all of us, he had to suffer the taunts of demons. If the Mystery of the Incarnation teaches me anything, it's that a holy life is not one that is absent of torment; rather, it is a life characterized by serenity in the face of torment.

You can live the Mystery of the Incarnation by developing a sense of serenity. Serenity, however, is not an objective or goal to achieve. Rather, it is a way of living in which one's sense of self-worth is not defined by what one achieves, but by a deep understanding that what will be will be and that all shall be well and good because God is always present.

Make time for purposelessness. That is, designate a period of time each day that is free from plans, objectives, or goals. Maybe sip a cup of coffee or tea slowly. Maybe go to a natural area and watch birds. Maybe go for a slow, meandering walk in a park. Distractions are a function of your own plans or agendas. When you are free of them, you will be free of distractions. Only then will you be open to God's will.

Nearness

Karl Rahner

1904–1984

Human beings seek nearness to one another. When they are in one another's direct physical presence and seek to love one another in these circumstances, they seek to exist not only in a physiological contact of flesh on flesh, but to render such contact, when it is to be meaningful, the expression of a really total, personal, fully mutual and reciprocal exchange of love between them. Here we have a mystery, that we cannot solve.

—Karl Rahner

Karl Rahner was one of the greatest theologians of the twentieth century. The German Jesuit wrote more books than I have read. He was appointed by Pope John XXIII to be an expert advisor for the Second Vatican Council. If you want to understand the development of Catholic philosophy and theology, Karl Rahner is required reading.

I tried reading Karl Rahner only to realize that maybe I shouldn't be reading Karl Rahner: he is way over my head. I didn't have a clue as to what he was talking about.

That got me thinking: if I can't understand Karl Rahner, how can I possibly hope to understand Jesus? Karl Rahner and I are not as separated as one might think. We lived during the same century. We both know German. I have been to Europe. I even know some Jesuits. But Jesus and me? We were separated by *thousands* of years. The only Aramaic word I know—*ephphatha* (which means "be opened")—I learned from Mark 7:34. And I've never been to the Holy Land. (Even my favorite film about Jesus was filmed in Tunisia.)

Plus, there's the fact that Jesus is the Son of God.

So, here's the crux of the problem: How can I claim or even imagine to be close to Jesus when he seems so distant? Can I really have a true relationship with him? And if so, how is that even possible? It's a mystery.

Karl Rahner offers me a helpful analogy. When I consider my relationship with my wife, Cathy, whom I love beyond reason (and whose love for me is utterly incomprehensible), I recognize that we remain distinct from each other. Even though we are often of one mind (we can finish each other's sentences), one heart (I know what she's feeling), and one body (read between the lines), we remain two separate individuals. Yet this is not a problem, Rahner explains, "For the lover loves and affirms the other precisely *as* other, certainly not seeking simply to absorb the beloved into his or her peculiar way of being."

That's something to ponder: if I believe that Jesus loves me, then that means Jesus loves me *as* me! Jesus is not trying to absorb me into God's self. God does not love a version of me who is not truly me. God loves me *as* me, as different and as distant as I am.

Suddenly, Jesus seems a lot closer, our love seems a lot more real, and finding God in all things seems all the more possible.

Awareness and Practice

The LORD is near to all who call on him,
to all who call on him in truth.

—Psalm 145:18

The Mystery of the Incarnation overcomes the problem of distance. Without the Incarnation, without the Word of God becoming fully human, God will never be anything more than an abstraction. You cannot get close to an abstraction. You cannot experience intimacy with an idea. But through the Incarnation, we can fall in love with and abandon ourselves to a person.

Pay attention to times throughout your day or week when God feels close to you or you feel close to God. Maybe you feel this closeness during prayer and liturgy. Maybe it's when you are with friends and family. Maybe God feels closest to you when you are in nature or when you are serving others. How would you describe those moments of closeness with God? What feelings well up inside you during those moments? Call out to God in those moments, because those are the times when God is calling out to you.

8

Intimacy

Bernard of Clairvaux

1090–1153

O happy kiss, and wonder of amazing self-humbling which is not a mere meeting of lips, but the union of God and man. The touch of the lips signifies the bringing together of souls.

—Bernard of Clairvaux

As I've gotten older, I've learned to appreciate music that I would have dismissed when I was younger. The music duo of Hall & Oates, for example, never would have been on my playlist twenty years ago, but now I have found myself cranking up the volume whenever I hear their songs. One of my favorites is "Kiss on My List."

I read an interview with Daryl Hall in which he explained that this was no ordinary love song. "It's an anti-love song," he said. "It means that your kiss is only on the list of the best things, it's not the *only* thing."

Like Hall & Oates, Bernard of Clairvaux—the Cistercian monk, theologian, preacher, and reformer who founded almost seventy monasteries, including the model community at Clairvaux—also sang about a kiss, but his song wasn't an anti-love song. Rather, his was the *ultimate* love song: the union between humanity and the Divine.

In a series of sermons on the Song of Solomon, Bernard describes the Mystery of the Incarnation as a kiss. In a kiss, there is the mouth that does the kissing, there is the person who gives the kiss, and the person who receives the kiss. Bernard identifies all three parts of the kiss with Jesus Christ: the mouth is the eternal Word that existed in the beginning with God and took on human nature (John 1:14), the person giving the kiss is the Son of God, and the person receiving the kiss is the man named Jesus.

Bernard also explains that we can return God's kiss. We begin by kissing God's feet. This is the kiss of repentance: "A truly humble desire to confess casts us down before him as if at his feet." Next, we kiss God's hand. This is the kiss of devotion, the desire to do more for God. Only after kissing God's hand can we kiss God on the lips, in which we find ourselves in the presence of God. This is the kiss of pure contemplation.

In looking for God in all things, we might begin with repentance, which is simply returning our gaze toward God. God lifts us from our lowly position, and we are filled with a burning love for God and neighbor. Holding God's hand, we are drawn to kiss God on the mouth, just like a couple on their wedding day.

Awareness and Practice

Let him kiss me with the kisses of his mouth!
For your love is better than wine,
your anointing oils are fragrant,
your name is perfume poured out;
therefore the maidens love you.

—Song of Solomon 1:1–4

The Incarnation is the kiss of peace between God and humanity. To live this mystery, we have to learn how to exchange the kiss of peace with others. We do this by seeking intimacy with others, that is, by building loving relationships that are embodied by closeness, sharing, trust, and safety.

Examine your relationships. Which ones embody closeness, sharing, trust, and safety? Which ones don't? What can you change in yourself to improve those relationships? Careful discernment is required here—some relationships are toxic, which limits what you can do without harming yourself.

What about your relationship with God? How would you describe that relationship? How important is your relationship with God? Is it one of many things that are all equally important, or is it the most important thing in your life? What obstacles prevent you from experiencing intimacy with God?

9

Motherhood

The Blessed Virgin Mary

First Century

My soul magnifies the Lord
and my spirit rejoices in God my Savior,
for he has looked with favor on the lowliness of his servant.
Surely, from now on all generations will call me blessed;
for the mighty One has done great things for me,
and holy is his name.

—Luke 1:46–49

Before I became Catholic, my wife took me to a talk given by Ivan Dragicevic, who, along with 5 others, claims that the Blessed Virgin Mary appeared to them beginning in 1981 in the village of Medjugorje, Bosnia-Herzegovina. According to Ivan and his companions, Mary came to "tell the world that God exists. He is the fullness of life, and to enjoy this fullness and peace, you must return to God." Four of them—including Ivan—claim to still receive messages from her at 6:40 p.m. every day.

In all honesty, I went to the talk skeptical and left even more so. In fact, I'm still skeptical about their witness; I'm not the kind of guy who believes stories about visions and apparitions of any kind. It also doesn't matter whether I believe them or not—the Church does not require that I believe in every revelation someone might have. But, like the Medjugorje visionaries and the millions who have been inspired by them, I have a very strong devotion to the Blessed Virgin Mary. Who knows? Maybe the seed for that devotion was planted that day when I heard Ivan Dragicevic share his story.

When I think of my devotion to the Blessed Virgin Mary, I realize that she is the mystic par excellence. Mysticism is traditionally defined as the experience of divine union. Mary had such intimacy with God that she gave birth to the Word made flesh. One of the trickier Catholic dogmas is that the Blessed Virgin Mary was redeemed from the moment of her conception; she was preserved from the effect of original sin. One way I wrap my brain around that dogma is that it explains her level of intimacy with God—from the moment of her conception, she was united to God, and a union through which the Second Person of the Trinity became flesh. If that doesn't describe divine union, nothing does.

Therein lies Mary's mystery: it's the mystery of motherhood. Mary's faith, her intimacy with God, made her mother to all the faithful because she gave birth to Jesus. As a result of her experience of divine union, Jesus came into the world—the Second Person of the Holy Trinity, without loss of his divinity, took on human flesh by being born of a human woman.

If I want to find God in all things, I will have to learn how to be a "mother" to Jesus, to give birth to him by making his presence known in everything I do or say, think or feel, hope for or desire. I will have to nourish him and raise him, care for him and console him. I will have to learn how to love someone—Jesus—more than I thought possible. Even though there might be times when I feel as if I'm failing at it (and even times when people tell me I am), I will continue to trust that I am loving him the best I can.

Sure, I may not be the best "mom" to Jesus. But who is?

Awareness and Practice

But when the fullness of time had come, God sent his Son, born of a woman, born under the law, in order to redeem those who were under the law, so that we might receive adoption as children.

—Galatians 4:4–5

We can live the Mystery of the Incarnation by first carrying the Lord in our hearts. Our heart then becomes a womb, where the Word once again takes on human flesh—our flesh. We can then give birth to the Mystery of the Incarnation through our holy activity.

Pay attention to your actions throughout the day. Which ones would you call holy? That is, which actions give praise and glory to God? How do these activities give birth to Christ through your flesh?

Look at the activities that you have not typically thought of as holy. How can you consecrate them? That is, in what ways can you see God acting through them?

10

Humility

Thomas à Kempis

c. 1380–1471

But if God be among us, we must at times give up our opinions for the blessings of peace. Furthermore, who is so wise that he can have full knowledge of everything? Do not trust too much in your own opinions, but be willing to listen to those of others.

—Thomas à Kempis

If we talk about politics, I will not hesitate to tell you how right I am and how wrong you are. Even if we agree, my reasons surely are better than yours.

In fact, it seems that my opinions are my greatest treasure.

Thomas à Kempis teaches in his little book *The Imitation of Christ* that opinions are dangerous things: "Differences of feeling and opinion often divide friends and acquaintances, even those who are religious and devout." Soapboxes are, after all, built from opinions.

Opinions inflate my ego and fill me with pride. According to Thomas, I tend to judge others not by truth but by my *opinions* about the truth. "We frequently judge that things are as we wish them to be, for through personal feeling true perspective is easily lost." Maybe that's why Jesus said, "Do not judge, and you will not be judged." (Luke 6:37) I do not have the perspective to judge things properly because my opinions keep getting in the way.

A long time ago, in a galaxy far away, another mystic said, "Your eyes can deceive you; don't trust them." Thomas à Kempis echoes Obi-Wan Kenobi: "our opinions, our senses often deceive us, and we discern very little."

So what can I do to free myself from my attachment to my opinions? Thomas suggests humility:

> "To think of oneself as nothing, and always to think well and highly of others is the best and most perfect wisdom. . . . All men are frail but you must admit that none is more frail than yourself."

Thomas isn't counseling self-loathing. Rather, he is counseling that we acknowledge our limitations. None of us knows as much as we think we know. There is always more to learn. Our opinions are at best incomplete, and more often than we care to admit, they are simply wrong.

Maybe that's the first step in finding God in all things: we must first liberate ourselves from our opinions, especially those about how God can and should act. We can find God in all things only when we no longer have an opinion about where to search for God. God is, after all, everywhere.

Awareness and Practice

Once when Jesus was praying alone, with only the disciples near him, he asked them, "Who do the crowds say that I am?" They answered, "John the Baptist; but others, Elijah; and still others, that one of the ancient prophets has arisen." He said to them, "But who do you say that I am?" Peter answered, "The Messiah of God."

—Luke 9:18–20

Peter's confession about Jesus tells us that to live the Mystery of the Incarnation is to recognize Jesus as the Messiah, the Christ. That's different from having an opinion about Jesus' identity. Opinions are poor substitutes for a lived faith. People's opinions about Jesus have led and likely will lead to arguments, heresies, and religious wars.

Imagine Jesus asking you: "But who do *you* say that I am?" What is your answer? Now, imagine Jesus challenging your answer. "That's just an opinion. How did you come to that opinion?" Continue this exchange to peel away all your opinions about who you *think* Jesus is until your only response is silence. Then rest with the Lord in that silence.

11

Apophasis

Dionysius the Areopagite

c. Fifth Century

The divinest and the highest of the things perceived by the eyes of the body or the mind are but the symbolic language of things subordinate to Him who Himself transcendeth them all.

—Dionysius the Areopagite

Apophasis is a Greek word meaning "negation" or "not saying." It is often used as a clever rhetorical device in which you say something other than what you mean (you can think of apophasis as a rhetorical relative of irony). For example, if my wife, Cathy, says to me, "I'm not calling you a jerk, but if I were, I'd say that you can be a real *a**hole*," she is using apophasis to tell me that I need to be kinder.

Apophasis is also used in theology. Whereas some theologians try to define or name what God is (which is called *kataphatic* theology, from the Greek word meaning "affirmation") by naming God's attributes—God is truth, God is beauty, God is goodness, etc.—apophatic theology names what God is *not*.

Dionysius the Areopagite was a Christian philosopher and theologian from the fifth or sixth centuries. He used apophatic theology in his short but powerful work *The Mystical Theology*. Dionysius describes apophatic theology as a process similar to carving a statue from marble: to see the image, the artist must chisel away all the material that hinders seeing the "hidden statue itself in its hidden beauty."

Our thoughts cannot fully comprehend the mysteries of God because they are finite, fleeting things (at the most basic level, a thought is an electrochemical impulse directed by the prefrontal cortex of the brain). God, in contrast, is infinite and eternal.

Not that our ideas and thoughts about God are not important—they are. Doctrine and dogma matter; they mediate and help us contemplate on the divine mysteries. There is just more to God than we can think of, *infinitely* more! But if we don't chisel away at our thoughts and ideas about God, they will simply become idols.

And perhaps that's a good way to think about how to find God: it's the art of stripping away what God is not until all that's left is God's unfathomable freedom.

Awareness and Practice

Let the same mind be in you that was in Christ Jesus,
who, though he was in the form of God,
did not regard equality with God
as something to be exploited,
but emptied himself,
taking the form of a slave.
And being born in human likeness.

—Philippians 2:6–7

The Incarnation is less a mystery to understand than a plan to implement: the plan of emptying one's self, of chiseling away at the marble of our thoughts and ideas about God to reveal the naked beauty of God who dwells in us.

Chisel away at your thoughts by observing them and then letting them go. When you find yourself absorbed in your thoughts, feelings, and opinions about God, others, yourself, or the world, say to yourself, "Not that" or "Not this." Rest in whatever is left; that's where you'll find God.

You can do the same thing with regard to the expectations you hold about your actions. When you think about your expected outcomes or hoped-for results, say the same thing: "Not this" or "Not that." Rest in whatever is left; that's where you'll find true freedom.

12

Interconnection

Pierre Teilhard de Chardin

1881–1955

And the Incarnation will be complete only when the part of chosen substance contained in every object—given spiritual import once in our souls and a second time with our souls in Jesus—shall have rejoined the final centre of its completion.

—Pierre Teilhard de Chardin

Pierre Teilhard de Chardin (1881–1955) fascinates me. He was a Jesuit priest, a geologist, and a paleontologist. For Chardin, science and faith could never be in conflict, since his faith informed his understanding of science and his scientific understanding informed his faith.

Of course, he had his detractors.

In 1962, Teilhard de Chardin's works were placed under a *monitum*—or warning—from the Vatican for "ambiguities and indeed even serious errors." He didn't get much love from his fellow scientists either: the Nobel laureate Peter Medawar thought his ideas were "nonsense, tricked out with a variety of tedious metaphysical conceits." Teilhard de Chardin seemed to be caught in the no-man's-land between the trenches in the ongoing war between faith and science.

Perhaps he found himself there because his search for God was inherently logical, and he approached it with the rigor of a scientist. Even his definition of *mystical union* sounds like something I would find in a science textbook: "the strengthening and purification of the reality and urgency contained in the most powerful interconnections revealed to us in every order of the physical and human world." In simpler terms, one can find God in all things because everything is connected.

Teilhard de Chardin summarized his approach to finding God using what he called the Divine Syllogism (a syllogism is a form of logical argument in which the conclusion follows naturally from the premises):

Each soul exists for God.
  All reality exists for our souls.
  All reality exists for God.

From his faith, he knew that each and every soul belongs to Christ, and from his years of field work digging up fossils, Teilhard de Chardin observed that everything is interconnected. "The human soul," he realized, "is inseparable . . . from the universe into which it was born." These premises led

Teilhard de Chardin to the conclusion that everything converges to a single point, and that point is Christ.

And that's why Pierre Teilhard de Chardin fascinates me: he shows me that we can find God in all things because everything is interconnected. Through our observation of the universe's unfolding from the Big Bang to the present, we see that we are all made of the same cosmic dust. Through our participation in the divine mysteries, we recognize that love—God—holds it all together.

Awareness and Practice

In the beginning was the Word, and the Word was with God, and the Word was God. He was in the beginning with God. All things came into being through him, and without him not one thing came into being.

—John 1:1–3

The Incarnation is not just a noun, it is a verb—a process. The Mystery of the Incarnation does not refer only to the birth of Jesus; rather, it describes the process through which God gathers all things into union with God. Through the process of the Incarnation, God permeates everything.

Consider the interconnectedness of all things. Ponder the fact that every subatomic particle in you, the things around you, and other people (even those who cause you stress) trace their source to the Big Bang fourteen billion years ago. You—along with everything that is, was, and ever will be—share the same cosmic fingerprint as the most ancient of fossils and the most brilliant of supernovas. Those are the fingerprints of God.

13

Convergence

Ilia Delio

b. 1955

Christogenesis means that evolution is not mere chance or random processes; it involves directed change, organized becoming, patterned process, and cumulative order.

—Ilia Delio

In her book *The Unbearable Wholeness of Being: God, Evolution, and the Power of Love,* the Franciscan sister and theologian Ilia Delio states that her "aim is to elucidate Christian life in an evolutionary world." In a footnote, she quotes a funny line from the journalist Robert Wright: "People who see a direction in human history, or in biological evolution, or both, have often been dismissed as mystics or flakes."

Which makes me wonder if this book needed a disclaimer: "WARNING: Reading this may result in your being dismissed, ignored, or rendered irrelevant."

Ilia Delio's theological research bridges the gap between science and religion, studying things like God and chaos theory, artificial intelligence, and prayer and quantum entanglement. But it's her ideas on Christ in evolution that interest me here.

Building upon the ideas of Pierre Teilhard de Chardin, Ilia Delio hypothesizes that God is the driver of the evolutionary process. At every stage in the development of the cosmos, God is "helping, driving, drawing" separate elements—from quarks to elephants—into greater union.

> Incarnation is not a separate event from creation but the act of creative personalization through unitive love. Love is the energy that empowers union; union generates new creation, and each new creation is more whole and united in love—more personal.

These words make me think about *the* Incarnation in a new way. It's not just a specific point in time, approximately two thousand years ago, when a person named Jesus was born in Bethlehem. The Incarnation is more than that: it is the recurring pattern for *all creation,* a sequence that continues to repeat itself, converging on the love modeled by Christ. God isn't just the "prime mover" as understood by medieval theologians, the one who got the whole thing started. Rather, God is creation's future—God is what all creation will become.

I'm dumbfounded: if God is the future of creation, and God is love, then the destiny of all created things is love. To find God in all things means falling in love with the universe, nothing more and nothing less.

That was Jesus' mission, Ilia Delio explains. Jesus brought together "those who were divided, separated, or left out of the whole. . . . He gathered together what was divided and confronted systems that diminished, marginalized, or excluded human persons."

He did so because that is what the universe will become.

Awareness and Practice

"And I, when I am lifted up from the earth, will draw all people to myself."

—John 12:32

The Mystery of the Incarnation is not contemplation of some event in the past; it is the contemplation of a future event, when all things are drawn by the power of love into union with one another. In that union, we will find God. You live the Mystery of the Incarnation by expressing that future love today. And what is love? Love is goodness giving itself away.

Recognize all that is good within you. What gives you life? Complete this sentence: "I am most alive when I . . ." When you have identified the good within you, ask yourself, *How do I give it away?* True love gives without asking anything in return. To whom will you give your goodness?

Part Two

The Paschal Mystery

I have a suspicion that suffering is a part of the human condition. Maybe that's a good way for me to think about original sin: it is the basic fact that human beings suffer simply because they are human. Jesus Christ, however, saves us from original sin not because he eliminates suffering but because, through the Paschal Mystery (Jesus' passion death, resurrection, and ascension), he teaches us the art of suffering well.

The mystics I chose to include in this part seem to have understood that distinction better than anyone else. Their lessons have helped me understand how I might learn to suffer well, because if I can find God in my suffering, then I can truly find God anywhere. I hope their stories and the practices I offer in this section will help you find and grow closer to God, even in times of trial, when God's presence might be harder to notice.

14

Suffering

Paul of the Cross

1694–1775

*Now is the moment to suffer in silence and in peace; resign yourself
to the agony you suffer, and it will conduct you to a mystical death.*

—Paul of the Cross

If God is omnipotent, omniscient, and perfectly good, then
why does God allow people to suffer?

Surely God, who is perfectly good, would prevent suffering.
Isn't that what goodness is all about? No suffering anywhere
in the world—no matter how small or insignificant—would
be unknown to God or hidden from God. And since God is
omnipotent, it is well within God's power to end it.

But suffering *does* exist; in fact, it is everywhere (just read
the morning newspaper). Therefore, God is either not all
knowing (he doesn't know about it), not all powerful (he can't
do anything about it), or not perfectly good (God can be a
jerk).

Some have sought to solve this dilemma by *theodicy* or the
reconciling of an omnipotent, omniscient, and perfectly good
God with the reality of evil and suffering. In this approach,

God uses suffering to build our character, as punishment, or to ensure that we are worthy to walk the straight and narrow path of the righteous.

Likewise, this approach seems to imply that God needs the devil: God is perfectly good and therefore would never inflict suffering. So God asks the devil to do the dirty work. No wonder the Rolling Stones tell us to have some sympathy for him.

However, St. Paul of the Cross—the Italian mystic who founded the Passionists—offers another insight about the question of suffering. It is the path to love:

> The soul that God would draw by means of prayer to a very close union with Himself ought, even in prayer, to pass by the way of suffering, of suffering divested of all consolation, the soul, in a certain sense, knowing not where she is; nevertheless, she understands, by the light infused into her from above, that she is always in the arms of her heavenly Spouse, sustained with the milk of His divine love.

St. Paul of the Cross is telling us that the existence of suffering isn't a dilemma because suffering is part of what it means to be human. Yes, evil exists—there are forces that cause people to suffer. Those forces may be mundane (the result of our own bad choices) or diabolic (the result of the devil's bad intentions). Suffering is a problem only when we believe that there is some reason we shouldn't suffer, when we ask the question, "Why me?!?" (The answer is, of course, "Why not you?")

The problem of suffering isn't that it exists. The real, practical problem of suffering is the temptation to try to avoid it altogether. Paul of the Cross teaches that we can find God even in our suffering—God's omnipotence, omniscience, and perfect goodness are revealed in the compassion we receive.

Awareness and Practice

May I never boast of anything except the cross of our Lord Jesus Christ, by which the world has been crucified to me, and I to the world.

—Galatians 6:14

We live the Paschal Mystery by uniting our individual suffering to Christ's universal suffering. When we live this mystery, we discover that none of us suffers alone; we all suffer with Christ.

Suffering is caused when your dreams, hopes, and deepest desires are being thwarted. Take a moment to examine an area of your life where you might be suffering. How are you suffering? This is the cross. Name the dreams, hopes, and deep desires that are being blocked. These are the nails that attach you to the cross. Do not try to escape them, simply acknowledge them and their relationship to your suffering.

As you experience the suffering of the cross, meditate on any (or all) of the following seven last words of Christ:

- "Father, forgive them; for they do not know what they are doing." (Luke 23:34)

- "Truly I tell you, today you will be with me in Paradise." (Luke 23:43)

- "Woman, here is your son. [Son], here is your mother." (John 19:26–27)

- "My God, my God, why have you forsaken me?" (Mark 15:34)

- "I am thirsty." (John 19:28)

- "It is finished." (John 19:30)

- "Father, into your hands I commend my spirit." (Luke 23:46)

How do you sense God's presence in these words?

15

Bridging

Catherine of Siena

1347–1380

I also wish you to look at the Bridge of My only-begotten Son, and see the greatness thereof, for it reaches from Heaven to earth, that is, that the earth of your humanity is joined to the greatness of the Deity thereby. I say then that this Bridge reaches from Heaven to earth, and constitutes the union which I have made with man.

—Catherine of Siena

Chicago has more movable bridges than any city in the world: there are fifty-two in the city, forty-three of which are still in operation. The most iconic design of these bridges is the trunnion bascule (a kind of bridge that pivots on an axle using counterweights), though other types of movable bridges in Chicago include the swing bridge, the vertical lift bridge, and the Scherzer lift bridge. All of these bridges were varied solutions to a single problem: how to allow people to cross the Chicago River without impeding ship traffic.

We face a similar problem in living the mysteries of our faith: how do we span the perceived gap between humanity and divinity without trying to swim across a river and getting pulled under by the wake of passing ships? Catherine of Siena understood that we need a bridge, and that bridge is Jesus Christ.

"There are three steps to the bridge," God the Father explains to Catherine in *The Dialog of Divine Providence*. "So the Bridge has three steps, in order that, climbing past the first and the second, you may reach the last, which is lifted on high, so that the water, running beneath, may not touch it." The first step of the bridge is *purgation*, that is, the soul strips itself of all vice. The second step is *illumination*, in which the soul is filled with virtue. The final step is *union*, in which the soul comes to know peace that surpasses all understanding. These steps are cemented together with the blood of Christ, and the bridge itself is covered with mercy.

The devil, however, has placed a Bridge Out sign on our side of the bridge, which is, of course, a lie. If we believe the lie, we might try one of three things. We might stay on this side of the river, we might try to build our own bridge, or we might try to swim across the river.

None of these are good ideas. First, to stay on this side of the bridge is to give up any hope of salvation, of union with God. To build our own bridge is no better—it will surely be unstable and will collapse under the slightest weight. To go under the bridge and swim the river that flows underneath it means certain death: "There are no stones," God the Father tells Catherine, "only water, and since there are no supports in the water, no one can travel that way without drowning."

The only way to find God, then, is to walk across this bridge: stripping ourselves of vices, growing in virtue, and trusting in God's mercy.

Awareness and Practice

Jesus said to him, "I am the way, and the truth, and the life. No one comes to the Father except through me."

—John 14:6

To live the Paschal Mystery means walking across the bridge of the cross. We have to strip ourselves of our vices. This can feel like a crucifixion because too often we think of our vices as virtues, and we would rather seek vengeance by calling it "justice" instead of extending mercy. But God the Father promises that "those who cross by the Bridge, being still in the darkness of the body, find light, and, being mortal, find immortal life, tasting, through love, the light of Eternal Truth."

Look carefully for each step of the bridge: of what vices do you need to be stripped? How do you see yourself growing in virtue? Where do you sense peace? What does mercy look like in your everyday life?

Whenever you practice mercy, you know you are walking on the bridge of the cross. While prayer helps us see the bridge, we have to decide to walk across it. Seeing our vices, we have to choose virtue. Seeing vengeance, we have to choose mercy.

16

Discontent

Hadewijch of Antwerp

Thirteenth Century

I wander alone and must remain far from him to whom I belong above all that I am, and for whom I would so gladly be perfect love. And—God knows—he has fruition of all, and I lack everything through which my soul might repose in him.

—Hadewijch of Antwerp

When I am at prayer, there are many times when I feel close to God. That feeling might have been fleeting, just a fraction of a flash of a bolt of lightning, but I know I felt what can only be called an overwhelming sense of peace and wholeness that would require a more talented writer to express. And yet, the darkness comes just as quickly, and I recognize that I'm even closer to all the things I wish I weren't: arrogance, suspicion, selfishness, and anger.

It's a painful gap, a chasm really, between the person I am when I know God's love and the person I am when I go about my everyday life.

"What's the deal, Lord?" I once asked. "Why am I left with such discontent?"

I imagined the Lord's answer: "It's because you think your contemplation comes to an end. Talk to Hadewijch about it."

The Lord was speaking about the great thirteenth-century poet, Beguine (women who lived in contemplative communities that were independent of monastic orders), and great mystic of love, Hadewijch of Antwerp.

So I read some of her letters, poems, and visions. If I understand Hadewijch correctly, my love for God is ever incomplete—loving God fills me with wonder and joy, but it leaves me always desiring God more. "According to this," Hadewijch wrote in a letter, "men on earth must strive for it with humble hearts and realize that, as regards such great love, and such sublime love, and this never-contented Beloved, they are too small to content him with love."

Thus, searching and finding God in all things will always leave us with a certain amount of discontent, a discontent that always calls us into greater union and greater intimacy with God. I suppose this insight helps me see discontent as something of a blessing, a revelation really: love of God always leads to a greater desire to love God. No wonder love of God and love of neighbor are linked. The more we love God, the more we want to love God, and the way we can fulfill that desire is to love all that God created. After all, we love the Creator by loving his creation.

That's why my contemplation never ends. I'm always left with a desire for greater union with God.

Awareness and Practice

I opened to my beloved,
    but my beloved had turned and was gone.
My soul failed me when he spoke.
I sought him, but did not find him;
    I called him, but he gave no answer.

—Song of Solomon 5:6

Our desire for mystical union with God can never be fully satisfied. No matter how much we yearn for it, we are left with some level of discontent. Perhaps this is a way to think about original sin. The Paschal Mystery overcomes our discontent because, through Jesus' suffering, we can see and experience what form love takes when God's love is fully satiated.

There are a few ways you can respond to any discontent you experience in your spiritual life.

- Respond with humility: recognize that discontent reveals the gap between you and God. Trust that God's love always spans that gap.

- Respond with devotion: renew your desire to love God all the more. Seek God's love in all things.

- Respond with purpose: let the renewed desire of your devotion be the only thing you seek in this world.

- Respond with detachment: discern your desires. Pursue only those that allow you to respond with humility, devotion, and purpose.

17

Grief

Margery Kempe

c. 1373–after 1438

Ever after this inspiration, she had in her mind the mirth and the
melody that was in Heaven, so much, that she could not well
restrain herself from speaking thereof, for wherever she was in any
company she would say oftentimes—"It is full merry in Heaven."
—*The Book of Margery Kempe*

On a Friday before one Christmas Day, Margery Kempe went to the Church of St. Margaret in Lynne in England. Dropping to her knees, she tearfully asked for God's mercy and forgiveness for her sins. At that point, Margery recorded the words the Lord shared with her:

Daughter, why weepest thou so sore? I am coming to thee, Jesus Christ Who died on the cross, suffering bitter pains and passions for thee I, the same God, forgive thee thy sins to the uttermost point. . . . Therefore I bid thee and command thee, boldly call Me "Jesus Christ, thy love," for I am thy love, and shall be thy love without end. And, daughter, thou hast a haircloth on thy back. I will that thou put it away, and I shall give thee a haircloth in thy heart that shall please Me much better than all the haircloths in the world.

Now, I know what a haircloth is. It's a garment made of coarse material such as animal hair (it's also known as a hair shirt or sackcloth). It would be worn next to the skin as a sign of mourning or penance. (Presumably, the irritation caused by the coarse fiber would reflect the interior pain and sorrow felt by the person wearing it.) Many people wore hair shirts in the Middle Ages as a way to resist temptation, which was probably why Margery wore one: she was tempted to commit adultery, only to be rejected by her would-be lover once she consented to sleep with him.

Jesus told Margery not to wear a haircloth next to her skin but next to her heart. Such a hair shirt is not made of coarse fiber; it's weaved from grief.

Perhaps what Jesus is telling me (through Margery, of course) is that I can find God by tending to my grief. If I can find God in my pain, sorrow, and suffering, then I will no longer run away or hide from those things. Grieving is not a sign of weakness. Nor is it simply a coping mechanism for negative emotions. Rather, grief is a source of wisdom if it's done in a healthy way. Grieving teaches us how to be present to our pain and sorrow so we can be present to the pain and sorrow of others, and that is the definition of compassion.

Awareness and Practice

He will wipe every tear from their eyes.
Death will be no more;
mourning and crying and pain will be no more,
for the first things have passed away.

—Revelation 21:4

The Paschal Mystery is a lesson in grief. It is also a reminder that grief leads to joy: the pain, suffering, and sorrow of Good Friday give way to the glory of Easter morning. Healthy grieving allows you to proclaim that it is "full merry in Heaven!"

When you experience the pain of loss, give yourself permission to grieve. Take a few deep breaths to ease the anxiety that may accompany your pain. Acknowledge your feelings. State explicitly what you are feeling: describe these feelings and locate them in your body. Let those feelings be there and sit with them without judgment—they are not "bad"; you are not "weak" or "wrong" for feeling them. Cry if you feel like it. Finally, show empathy. Say to yourself, *Yes, I hurt, and even though I am hurting, I love myself.*

Long-lasting or debilitating grief may be a sign of something more serious. If you experience this, seek professional or medical help so you can share and process your emotions with closer guidance and, most importantly, heal.

18

Hope

Maria Esperanza Bianchi

1928–2004

There has been pain in my soul, but there has been joy too. The immense joy that the Lord has led me softly, with grief but also with joy and satisfaction. I have no means of compensating all the warmth and the love He has given my beloved ones and me.

—Maria Esperanza Bianchi

Meg Griffin, the oft-maligned daughter in the cartoon series *Family Guy*, offered the following definition of hope:

Hope is what gets you out of bed in the morning when it's the day of prom and you haven't been asked. Hope pushes the caterpillar through the cocoon and drives the salmon upstream. . . . Hope is a horizon we head for, leaving nothing behind us but fear. And though we may never reach our goals, it's hope that will save us from who we once were.

It's inspiring, I suppose, but it doesn't help me with the fact that there are times when I can't get out of bed because I feel so depressed and life is so devoid of meaning that getting up feels pointless. What does hope look like for me then? Sure, I may be like the salmon swimming upstream, except that the river I'm swimming in has been dammed. What drives me then? What will save me from who I once was when I don't even want to know who I am?

"Don't give up hope," you may say. Well, I reply, "Save your platitude for someone else, someone like the Venezuelan mystic and visionary Maria Esperanza Bianchi."

If anyone had a reason not to be hopeful, Maria did. One of five children, her father died when she was only two years old. When her older brother, who supported the family, died a few years later, Maria was the one who had to go buy the coffin. At age twelve, she developed pneumonia and the doctors gave her only a few days to live. After a vision from the Blessed Virgin Mary, she was miraculously healed. Two years later, she fell ill again—this time it was her heart, and the doctors gave her only hours to live. Divine intervention spared her again. This became the pattern of her life.

Maria always had hope because she experienced many deaths, each of which was followed by a resurrection. For her, the Paschal Mystery wasn't about theology; it was her way of life.

But what about those of us who never experience the joy of Easter, only the despair of Good Friday? What does hope look like for us?

Perhaps hope is not the idea that I *can* find God, but simply the desire that I *want* to find God. I like thinking about hope that way, because now I don't have to worry about finding God in my desolation—that may be asking too much of me. Instead, all I need is the desire to experience God's love in those dark moments.

Awareness and Practice

LORD of hosts, restore us;
   let your face shine upon us,
   that we may be saved.

—Psalm 80:8

We can easily believe in the Paschal Mystery because we know how the story ends: we know that there was the glory of Easter morning following the desolation of Good Friday. Jesus' disciples didn't know that Jesus was going to rise again; all they had was the sadness from having witnessed his death. What did they do?

You can live the Paschal Mystery by sitting with your desolation, not running from it or wishing it away, just as Mary Magdalene did, sitting at the tomb where Jesus was buried (see Matthew 27:61). As you sit with your desolation, express your desire to know God's love in that moment. You can recite the psalm above (or write your own); you can listen to music that encapsulates your feelings. You can cry and offer your tears to God. You can also sit in silence.

You can also live this mystery by offering your presence to people who are experiencing desolation.

19

Heartfulness

Clare of Montefalco

c. 1268–1308

If you are looking for Christ's cross, take my heart. You will find the suffering Lord there.

—Clare of Montefalco

At my last physical, my doctor told me that my heart rate was abnormally low.

"That's because I'm in great shape!" I said.

She looked at my chart and shook her head. "We'd better do an EKG."

After the nurse attached me to bundles of wires connected to the machine that graphically recorded the electrical activity of my heart, my doctor looked at the readout and said, "Huh. That's weird." She referred me to a cardiologist who ordered an ultrasound to get an image of my heart. During the ultrasound I looked at the screen and shouted in excitement, "Look! I have two hearts! I must be a Time Lord!" (Whovians—fans of the British sci-fi show *Doctor Who*—know that Time Lords have two hearts.)

"You don't have two hearts," the technician said. "I just have two images of your heart on the screen."

While I was disappointed that I wasn't an alien who could master time and relative dimension in space, I was relieved that my cardiologist found nothing irregular in my heart.

St. Clare of Montefalco, on the other hand, did have an abnormality with her heart. After her death, the sisters of the monastery where she was abbess removed her heart to put it in a reliquary (not an uncommon practice in her day, especially for holy women such as Clare). They noticed that her heart bore an image of the cross of Christ. They even found a miniature lance inside it.

There are few images more important than that of the heart. The heart represents the place where God encounters the human soul. In other words, the heart is *the place* where we find God. I know that my heart was not imprinted with the cross of Christ, and I know that there were no metal objects in it. Maybe that was why I wished I had two hearts—not because I wanted to be an alien but because that would have increased the probability that one of them would have been marked with a sign of Christ's passion.

But I have only one heart. And maybe that's the question I have to ask myself—which is the question that all of us have to ask: when we look deep into our heart, will we find God there?

Awareness and Practice

Keep your heart with all vigilance,
   for from it flow the springs of life.

—Proverbs 4:23

You live the Paschal Mystery by bearing the cross of Christ in your heart. While this entails the awareness of another person's suffering, it also entails the hope of the resurrection—that their suffering will be transformed into the glory of the resurrected Christ. This compassion is the essence of a practice called *heartfulness*.

Here's how you can practice heartfulness. First, connect with your heart. Notice its location in your chest, its rhythmic beating. When you locate this space, imagine it expanding outward. Open this space to take in the suffering in the world—suffering that is both personal and impersonal. Let that suffering rest within your heart.

As you go about your day, continue to pay attention to your heart. Assess the extent to which it is shut off to the rest of the world and the extent to which it is open to it. You can do this by looking at your actions: do they reflect a heart that is open or one that is closed? When you find that your heart seems closed, open it a little bit, and watch how your actions change. Then see if you can open it a little more.

20

Disappointment

Francis of Assisi

1182–1226

The Lord gave me, Brother Francis, thus to begin doing penance in this way: for when I was in sin, it seemed too bitter for me to see lepers. And the Lord Himself led me among them and I showed mercy to them. And when I left them, what had seemed bitter to me was turned into sweetness of soul and body. And afterwards I delayed a little and left the world.

—Francis of Assisi

One day I was meditating on Jesus being mocked by soldiers, crowning him with thorns, when I noticed myself humming the Metallica song "King Nothing." In the music video, a man dressed as a king wanders around a snowy forest, discarding the crown he is wearing before picking up and putting on another one, again and again and again. By the end of the video, there are crowns *everywhere*.

I began to think of myself in that video. Each crown represents an expectation I have of myself (or an expectation someone has of me), and every time I face disappointment, when I fail to meet that expectation, I toss it aside. Then I pick up another crown—I set another expectation—and sure enough, I'm met with another disappointment. On and on it goes. My life is littered with the discarded crowns of failed expectations.

And that's when I thought of St. Francis of Assisi.

His path was littered with discarded crowns too. Francis wanted to be a famous knight known for his bravery on the battlefield. In the only battle he fought, he was captured and held captive for a year. When Francis went to join the army of Walter of Brienne and fight in the Crusades, he had a vision of a room filled with knightly arms and trophies. Thinking that this was confirmation of his knightly desires, he was told otherwise. "Go back the way you came," a voice told him.

Unlike me, Francis gave up chasing crowns all together. The only crown he sought was the crown of thorns worn by Christ. Thomas of Celano, Francis's first biographer, writes that Francis "began to consider himself less and less, until by the mercy of the Redeemer, he came to complete victory over himself."

Expectations are really only expressions of my will, and disappointment results when my will is thwarted. Perhaps that's what Francis is trying to teach me: I can find God in my disappointment because that's the only place where I will find victory over my own will.

Awareness and Practice

The soldiers led him into the courtyard of the palace (that is, the governor's headquarters); and they called together the whole cohort. And they clothed him in a purple cloak and twisting some thorns into a crown, they put it on him. And they began saluting him, "Hail, King of the Jews!" They struck his head with a reed, spat upon him.

—Mark 15:16–20

At first glance, the Paschal Mystery makes Jesus look like the God who failed. Too often, we wear our disappointments and failures like a crown of thorns. But the Paschal Mystery reminds us that the crown of thorns is really a crown of glory, because it represents the complete submission to God's will. And that is precisely where living this mystery will lead us.

To help you live this mystery, identify an expectation that you currently have. How would you feel if you fulfilled that expectation? How would you react if you didn't? Now imagine that you never had that expectation. What would your reaction be if that former expectation were realized? And what if it weren't? What difference do you notice in those reactions?

For the detached person—one who is truly free—there would be no difference in their reaction. That kind of freedom is required if you truly want to live God's will and not your own.

21

Affliction

Rita of Cascia

1377–1457

She, too, was become an outcast from amongst men, but instead of being afflicted thereby, she was only the more strongly united to God.

—*The Life of Saint Rita of Cascia*

A spider once bit me in the middle of my forehead.

At first I thought it was just a mosquito bite, but then it began to swell to the point in which I knew everyone could see it. It got worse: pus began to ooze from it. For a week and a half, it would scab over, then the scab would fall off, and the sore would continue to ooze pus. A small hole was beginning to develop in my forehead, and the right side of my face started to swell up.

I must have looked like an abomination. Even though it was there for everyone to see, nobody ever mentioned the big, oozing welt on my head. (You know something obvious is really gross when people choose to ignore it.)

Nobody has ever liked having a big, gross mark on their face, except maybe St. Rita of Cascia. The Augustinian nun had a great devotion to Christ's passion. One day, in 1443, she received a "seal of merit": a wound on her forehead that looked as if she had been pierced by a thorn. The partial stigmata remained with her for years. It became infected and infested with worms. (The worms would actually fall from the sore; she called them her "little angels.")

And while I bore my fester with shame, Rita embraced her wound with joy. She never ceased blessing, thanking, and praising Christ for it. Her wound was a gift that kept on giving—not worms, but grace.

I imagine it must have been hard to talk to St. Rita with such an ulcer on her face. I know I would have turned my gaze away from her.

I find it hard to look at other people's wounds. I want wounds to be out of sight and out of mind. Maybe I'll look away. Maybe I'll say, "It's not that bad" or "It will get better." Maybe I'll blame the person for his or her wound, as if it were a natural (or just) consequence of bad behavior. For whatever reason—maybe they make me feel weak and vulnerable—I prefer blindness when it comes to seeing another person's wounds. I suspect that I'm not alone in this.

But Jesus came to give sight to the blind (see Luke 4:18). Perhaps the divine sight he gives us is not supposed to help us see only his glory but rather to see how other people are hurting so we can offer compassion.

Maybe that's exactly where we're supposed to see the fullness of God's glory: in the compassion we offer others.

Awareness and Practice

He was despised and rejected by others;
  a man of suffering and acquainted with infirmity;
and as one from whom others hide their faces
  he was despised, and we held him of no account.

—Isaiah 53:3

To live the Paschal Mystery means finding beauty in the ugliness of Jesus' wounds. But when we look at a crucifix, we usually see Jesus with six-pack abs and covered in a loincloth—not a humiliated and naked Jesus with a distended stomach and covered in blood and dirt. We forget that in turning our eyes away from Jesus' bloodied, broken body, we have turned our gaze away from God himself.

Perhaps the best place to enter the Paschal Mystery is to acknowledge whatever afflicts you personally. Those afflictions may be physical, psychological, emotional, or spiritual. Name them and gently say, "Hello. You are welcome. I will take care of you." As you spend time with your afflictions, listen closely to them. Their wisdom will guide you to understand how to care for them.

Once you know how to listen to and care for your own wounds, you will learn how to listen to and care for the wounds of others, because all suffering speaks the same language of God's mercy and compassion.

22

Tragedy

Marguerite Porete

c. Thirteenth Century–1310

Then appeared the Land of Freeness, and there Justice came to me,
and asked me what sort of clemency I wished from her. And I
answered her, such as I was, that I wished no clemency from her,
nor from anything which could torment me.

—Marguerite Porete

There will always be people who think that God can be found
only in *certain* things—things we call *holy* or *sacred*. To say
that God can be found in *all* things, however, that might be
too much for them. If that were the case, where would the
boundary be between what is holy and unholy? Where would
the boundary be between what is sacred and secular? No—to
find God in all things would be just too much. It would lead
to heresy.

Unfortunately, a lot of people insist on enforcing hard bor-
ders between a realm they call Good and a realm they call
Wicked. They want to build a wall, as if God needs *our*
protection. Anyone who dares climb over that wall is liable to
get burned at the stake.

That's what happened to the Beguine mystic Marguerite Porete.

She wrote her book *The Mirror of Simple Souls* "so that you might hear in order to be more worthy of the perfection of life and the being of peace to which the creature is able to arrive through the virtue of perfect charity." Even though she had her book reviewed and approved by three authorities, including Godfrey of Fontaines, who was one of the preeminent theologians of the day, Marguerite freely admitted its shortcomings: "For it is a difficult book to understand," she wrote. "Theologians and other clerks," she warned, "you will not have the intellect for it."

Maybe that last line is what got her into trouble.

The bishop of Cambrai, Guy of Colmieu, had her book burned while Marguerite stood and watched. In March of 1310, William of Paris, the personal confessor of King Philip IV of France and inquisitor of France, convened a panel of theologians to examine Marguerite and her book. (Coincidentally, William of Paris had also directed King Philip IV's campaign against the Knights Templar.) By April, *The Mirror of Simple Souls* was condemned as heretical. In May, another panel—this one made up of canon lawyers—declared that Marguerite was a relapsed heretic because she refused to answer questions during her trial and because she ignored Guy of Colmieu's injunction against speaking in public about her book. On June 1, she was burned at the stake. Throughout her whole ordeal, Marguerite remained silent.

Marguerite's story is tragic, and it offers an important lesson about the quest to find God: it makes a lot of people uncomfortable, especially those who think of themselves as responsible for deciding where and when God can be found.

Awareness and Practice

"When they bring you before the synagogues, the rulers, and the authorities, do not worry about how you are to defend yourselves or what you are to say; for the Holy Spirit will teach you at that very hour what you ought to say."

—Luke 12:11–12

Jesus suffered silently. He didn't argue. He didn't make his case.

He knew what was in store for him. When given chances to defend himself—before Caiaphas and the Sanhedrin, before Pontius Pilate—he said nothing. He did this because he had surrendered his life to the will of his heavenly Father.

You live the Paschal Mystery when you suffer as Jesus did: quietly and without argument. The arguments you make to defend yourself more likely reflect your own will and desires, not God's.

Reflect on times when you have been condemned or attacked. How did you respond? With forceful counterarguments? With silence? Imagine how you would respond if you did so with complete trust in God the Father's will instead of your own.

When you face condemnation or hostile criticism in the future—or when you direct it toward others—stop and be quiet. That will open up the space for God's mercy to prompt your response.

23

The True Self

Thomas Merton

1915–1968

Ultimately, the only way that I can be myself is to become identified with Him in Whom is hidden the reason and fulfillment of my existence.

—Thomas Merton

My spiritual director once instructed me in a very difficult practice.

"Ask yourself, *Who am I?* And then, whatever answer you give, negate it by saying, 'No, that is not who I am. That is a label. Who is the person with that label?'"

For example, if I answer the question *Who am I?* by saying, "I am Bob Burnham," my response would be "No, that is not who I am. That is the name I was given. Who is the person with that name?"

If I answer, "I am a human being," I negate that too, saying, "No, that is not who I am. That is my species. Who is this particular human being?"

I repeat this process and stop not when I've found an answer, but when I've learned how to rest.

I have a feeling that Thomas Merton (1915–1968) would have loved this meditation. The Trappist monk and poet might call whatever answers I come up with for my false selves, "the man I want to be but who cannot exist because God does not know anything about him." Like the Invisible Man, who wrapped himself in bandages so that he could be seen, I wrap myself in the bandages of my experiences and ideas because *I* want to be seen, recognized, and respected. The problem, Merton warns, is that I confuse the bandages for the man: "A life devoted to the cult of this shadow is what is called a life of sin."

Who then, is my *true self?*

Merton offers a simple answer: "Love is my true identity. Selflessness is my true self. Love is my true character. Love is my name." Merton also tells me where to find my true self: "To find love I must enter the sanctuary where it is hidden, which is the mystery of God."

The entrance into that sanctuary is, of course, the cross of Christ. To find my true self, I have to die: I have to unwrap the bandages and be willing to look into an empty space and see nothing. The person I thought I was, in reality, is not a person or thing at all. It was just an illusion. When you pierce the veil of the illusion, you will find God rejoicing in your true self.

Awareness and Practice

Then Jesus told his disciples, "If any want to become my followers, let them deny themselves and take up their cross and follow me. For those who want to save their life will lose it, and those who lose their life for my sake will find it."

—Matthew 16:24–25

Jesus is clear: discipleship is not about claiming membership to the country club of salvation. Quite the contrary. Discipleship means embracing the Paschal Mystery: you must pick up the cross and die to the false self. Whatever you think you are, you are not—you are God's mystery: ineffable and unknowable, but infinitely loved by God.

Ask yourself, *Who am I?* Negate the answer—whatever it is, no matter how good or bad it may be, it is not you. Repeat this question and negate each answer until only silence remains. As you do this meditation, you may find that some things are harder to negate than others—maybe it's your job, your political affiliation, or your role in a relationship. Take note of these, because these are the hard attachments that prevent you from realizing your true self.

24

Darkness

John of the Cross

1542–1591

In order that God lift the soul from the extreme of its low state to the other extreme of the high state of divine union, He must obviously, in view of these fundamental principles, do so with order, gently, and according to the mode of the soul.

—John of the Cross

I like to imagine myself having conversations with Jesus. One time, Jesus interrupted me and said, "You know you're just talking to yourself, right?"

What a buzzkill. I love using my imagination—just as the physical senses of taste, touch, smell, sight, and hearing help me interact with the physical world, my imagination is a mental sense that helps me interact with the spiritual world.

St. John of the Cross explains the problem with interactions that rely on the senses. "If something is spiritual," he wrote in *The Ascent of Mount Carmel*, "it is incomprehensible to the senses; but if the senses can grasp it, it is no longer spiritual." Knowledge of God, he explains, "never deals with particular things, since its object is the Supreme Principle.

Consequently, one cannot express it in particular terms." So if I understand the Spanish friar correctly, the "conversations" I imagine having with Jesus are not real, because if I were *really* talking to God, the experience would be beyond anything I could imagine, since such an experience transcends anything my mind *could possibly* comprehend!

In other words, I have to enter a kind of darkness where I have to feel my way toward God without relying on any of my physical (or mental) senses.

Well that's frustrating. No wonder his Carmelite brothers threw him in prison—not because they opposed his efforts to reform the Carmelite order but because his teachings about spirituality were annoying. We are, after all, physical creatures. Our senses are the interface between ourselves and the world in which we exist, including the spiritual world.

St. John did not discount our senses, however. God communicates to us through them so that we "may form a habit in spiritual things." But such communication is only the first step in a process. To grow in life with God, St. John taught that we must divest ourselves of our senses until our spirit no longer pays attention to them. To make this even harder, this divestiture is something we cannot do—only God can—and it happens on God's own timetable, not our own.

And perhaps this is the lesson St. John offers me: I need to learn how to find God in what he called the "dark night of senses," that is, I have to go beyond trusting in my ability to sense God in this, that, or some other thing, because God is *nada*, or no "thing" at all.

Awareness and Practice

My God, my God, why have you forsaken me?
  Why are you so far from helping me, from the words of my
    groaning?
O my God, I cry by day, but you do not answer;
  and by night, but find no rest.

—Psalm 22:1–2

The Paschal Mystery invites you to enter the dark night of the senses, to look past your feelings, your desires, and your motivations in everything you do—no matter how holy it may seem—and be drawn into the *more* of God.

There may be times when you may have difficulty sensing the nearness of God. What grounds your faith during such times of darkness? How do you remember the experience of hope in those moments? Sometimes, probing the darkness of God's absence can reveal that God is closer to you than you could have imagined, operating in secret or under the surface of your conciousness.

Since exploring the dark side of your spirituality can be a difficult and troubling process, you may want to work with a trained spiritual director who can guide you as you explore it more deeply. Be sure to consult one if what you find is consistently troubling.

25

Continuity

Catherine of Genoa

1447–1510

My soul seems to live in this body as in a purgatory which resembles the true purgatory, with only the difference that my soul is subjected to only so much suffering as the body can endure without dying, but which will continually and gradually increase until death.

—Catherine of Genoa, *Treatise on Purgatory*

Time for a brief math lesson:

A function f is said to be **continuous** at a point c if

$$\lim_{x \to c} f(x) = f(c).$$

Think of it this way: a continuous function is a curve that you can draw without lifting your pencil off a sheet of paper.

This concept of continuity helps me understand the doctrine of purgatory. The Catholic Church teaches that when people die in God's grace but were not perfect at the time of their death (that's pretty much all of us), God will purify them so they can achieve the holiness necessary to enter into the Divine presence.

In the *Life and Doctrine of Saint Catherine of Genoa*, Catherine explains a vision she had of purgatory:

> I see that as far as God is concerned, paradise has no gates, but he who will may enter. For God is all mercy, and his open arms are ever extended to receive us into his glory. But I see that the divine essence is so pure—purer than the imagination can conceive—that the soul, finding in itself the slightest imperfection, would rather cast itself into a thousand hells than appear, so stained, in the presence of the divine majesty. Knowing, then, that purgatory was intended for her cleaning, she throws herself therein, and finds there that great mercy, the removal of her stains.

Purgatory is not so much a place as it is the process of purification. And that process is a continuous one: each and every moment of my life here on earth is drawn by God toward heaven. On the one hand, I am enough for God, and I'm left asking myself, as Catherine did, "What am I that God seems truly to have no care for any one but me?" This brings me a peace that is unlike anything save that of, as Catherine tells me, the saints in heaven.

On the other hand, I am called to love God with nothing less than the same love with which God loves me. And that, Catherine explains, can be terrifying because it is greater than anything I can imagine.

Catherine teaches me that there is no barrier between heaven and earth; there are no hoops to jump through in finding God, no fences to jump over. There is just the continuous process of loving God more and more. It's as if God is drawing a line from your heart to Jesus' heart without ever having to lift his pencil off the paper.

Awareness and Practice

And through him God was pleased to reconcile to himself all things, whether on earth or in heaven, by making peace through the blood of his cross.

—Colossians 1:20

One of the greatest temptations we face is thinking that no matter how much we love God, our love is not ever going to be enough. There will always be a gap between our love and God's. Our love is, in a sense, not continuous. However, Jesus filled that gap by dying on the cross. The gap exists only in our thinking mind.

To live the Paschal Mystery is to learn how to let God's grace perfect our love as it flows freely between our heart and Jesus' heart unobstructed.

At times, when my imperfect nature is at the forefront of my mind, the only way I know to tap into that flow is to be like the criminal who hung at Jesus' side at Golgotha and asked for God's mercy (see Luke 23:39–43). Perhaps repeating his words as a simple mantra, "Jesus, remember me when you come into your kingdom," is all you need, or can muster, in times like those. As you hang from the cross of your imperfections, let Christ's sacrifice fill you with his infinite and perfect love.

Part Three

The People of God

The mystics I present in this part remind me of a fundamental fact: faith is communal. We do not look for God on our own; rather, it's a search we can conduct only with others. Yes, we are all called to a personal relationship with Jesus Christ, but we are also called to more: we are called to a relationship with Christ that is found only in community.

This is the Mystery of the People of God: we find God in our relationships with others—and not just with other people, but with all creation. In those relationships, we build a community. This community is more than just people who share the same beliefs. It is a community built upon love. I hope the stories and practices in this section will help you build such communities and thrive in them.

26

Covenant

Abraham

c. early Second Millennium B.C.

Then Abram fell on his face; and God said to him, "As for me, this is my covenant with you: You shall be the ancestor of a multitude of nations. No longer shall your name be Abram, but your name shall be Abraham; for I have made you the ancestor of a multitude of nations."

—Genesis 17:3–5

The Seventh Generation Principle is an idea that can guide sustainability: we need to consider the impact our use of the earth's natural resources will have on the next seven generations. This principle finds its inspiration from the Great Law of the Haudenosaunee (also known as the Iroquois Confederacy):

> Look and listen for the welfare of the whole person and have always in view not only the present but also the coming generations, even those whose faces are yet beneath the surface of the ground—the unborn of the future Nation.

The Seventh Generation Principle reminds me that I have promises to keep. I have responsibilities toward the seventh generation: I will look to their welfare. I can do this by living in a sustainable manner—Sister Mother Earth's resources, while vast, are finite. Am I supporting policies that encourage rapid depletion for quarterly profits? Similarly, am I supporting policies that prevent the next generation from being born?

I also have responsibilities toward the generations who came before me, the generations who thought of me when my face was yet beneath the surface of the earth. Earlier generations have gathered valuable wisdom, and their traditions speak that wisdom. Am I willing to learn and respect those traditions?

This promise is a covenant, and to help me understand the nature of this covenant, I can look at the covenant God made with Abraham, the patriarch of the three great monotheistic religions—Judaism, Christianity, and Islam. The covenant between God and Abraham is a promise of divine favor and grace in exchange for exclusivity: humanity is for God and God is for humanity. God's part of the covenant is divine union. Our part of the covenant is to find God.

This covenant is a communal one. It wasn't just a promise made between Abraham and God; it was a covenant between Abraham and all his descendants. The promise Abraham made is a promise that I am expected to keep, it's a promise I'm expected to make myself, and it's one I'm to make for the generations that follow. Our obligations to God are not relics of some mythic past; they are lived today and preserved for generations yet to come. I fulfill those obligations by learning the wisdom and traditions of my elders and by seeing the hope and promise of today's young people.

I'm sure I'll find God there.

Awareness and Practice

But Jesus has now obtained a more excellent ministry, and to that degree he is the mediator of a better covenant, which has been enacted through better promises.

—Hebrews 8:6

We can live the Mystery of the People of God by recognizing our responsibilities and obligations required under the covenant God made through Jesus Christ. The terms of this new covenant are easy to understand: to love God and love your neighbor. However, these terms are not always easy to fulfill.

How well do you live up to the requirements of this new covenant? Do you find yourself limiting your definition of who God is, who your neighbors are, and what love actually requires of you? In what ways is your love conditioned on particular images of or ideas about God or concepts of people's worthiness?

After you have identified those limitations, discern ways God is calling you to expand your understanding about what the true requirements of love are and how you might fulfill them. Ask for whatever grace you need to let go of old patterns of thinking, acting, and being so you can love others as Jesus loves you.

27

Pacifism

John Paul II

1920–2005

"No to war! War is not always inevitable. It is always a defeat for humanity. . . . War is never just another means that one can choose to employ for settling differences between nations."

—John Paul II

On January 3, 2020, the United States of America killed Iranian Major General Qasem Soleimani in a drone attack in Baghdad, Iraq. Five days later, Iran launched ballistic missiles at two U.S. air bases in Iraq. I was worried that we were going to end up in another war in the Middle East that would lead to chaos, misery, and death.

Of course, one could make the argument that we weren't acquiescing to another war, just continuing the one we started in 2003, when we invaded Iraq.

Pope John Paul II vehemently opposed that war: "War cannot be decided upon, even when it is a matter of ensuring the common good, except as the very last option and in accordance with very strict conditions, without ignoring the consequences for the civilian population both during and after the military operations." His words came to my mind as I waited to hear whether or not President Trump would retaliate for Iran's missile attack.

I tend to overlook John Paul II for a lot of reasons, but during the first few weeks of 2020, I came to appreciate the man who, despite many failings, helped defeat communism in Poland and the Soviet Union without firing a single shot. John Paul II reminds us that we have to do more than listen to a song by another John, *Give peace a chance!* We have to make peace our way of life.

If we look seriously at the consequences of war on civilian populations during and after a war, we will see only chaos, misery, and destruction. We should have learned by now that war can never be a choice—we can never *discern* whether to go to war or not because war is never good. It is never a *good* option.

John Paul II teaches me that I need to imagine a new world that Christ would recognize. It's a world where strength and power are measured by our collective heart—that is, our ability as a people to forgive, reconcile, and heal—and not by the size and sophistication of our military. It's a world where we judge people not by the injury they can inflict but by their potential for goodness. It's a world that says the life of the enemy has as much dignity as the life of a friend. In short, it's a world that lives in peace.

Yes, it's a beautiful dream, and some people may say it's naive, impractical, or even dangerous. But it's a dream in which I am certain we will find God.

Awareness and Practice

When those who were around him saw what was coming, they asked, "Lord, should we strike with the sword?" Then one of them struck the slave of the high priest and cut off his right ear. But Jesus said, "No more of this!" And he touched his ear and healed him.

—Luke 22:49–51

To live the Mystery of the People of God, we must learn to be peacemakers. We must learn to reject violence and embrace healing.

We can start by recognizing the dignity of all people. That means accepting that people have the right to be as they are. Begin by reflecting on your interactions throughout the day. Are you wishing that people were somehow different? If you are, then you are committing a subtle act of violence.

Second, we must trust people. People will learn to trust us if we give them our trust. What are situations when it is easy to trust others? What are situations when it is hard to trust others? What grace do we need to be trusting and trustworthy?

Finally, we need to be concerned about the health and happiness of others. Such solidarity will build fraternity with others. How can we show others our concern for their health and happiness?

By respecting all people, trusting others (even when it's hard), and showing concern, we will see the futility of violence and free ourselves from the idea that it is ever justified.

28

Irrationality

Marie de l'Incarnacion

1599–1672

*I was leaving more, in leaving my son whom I loved very much,
than if I had left all imaginable possessions, and above all, leaving
him without support.*

—Marie de l'Incarnacion

Let's play a game.

Imagine that I have given you ten dollars. You can either keep all the money for yourself, or you can share it with an anonymous individual. What do you do? Take a moment to think about it.

Did you decide to keep all the money for yourself? Congratulations! You acted in a rational, self-interested way.

Did you give some of it away? Then you acted in a way that can be called *reasonable*. A growing body of research suggests that human beings are more often reasonable than rational—people, in fact, are more likely to choose to act irrationally.

The difference between rationality and reasonableness helps me make sense of the troubling story of the French mystic Marie de l'Incarnacion.

Marie had always wanted to be a nun, but her parents had other ideas and arranged for her to be married to a silk merchant. He died in 1619, two years after they were wed, leaving Marie a widow—and a mother. Nevertheless, in 1631, Marie entered the Ursuline monastery in Tours, abandoning her son, Claude.

The choice tore her up—"it seemed to me I was being split in half," she would write later. Nor was it easy on Claude (he made repeated attempts to demand the Ursulines return his mother to him—he even assembled a mob to besiege the Ursuline monastery). Then, in 1633, she had a dream that she interpreted to mean that she should be a missionary in Canada. She would abandon her son again.

Now I know Jesus said that you cannot be his disciple if you don't "hate" your family (see Luke 14:26), but I don't think that gives you permission to abandon your child. It seems irrational.

But we are *reasonable* creatures, not *rational* ones. Reasonable people are guided by norms of fairness that go beyond cold logic. When I think someone is acting irrationally, they may be acting reasonably, and I'm just ignorant of how they might differentiate between what is fair and unfair. Marie de l'Incarnacion had a total commitment to Christ; that was the standard of fairness she lived by.

I'm not in a position to defend or condemn Marie's decision to abandon her son. (Claude later came to understand why his mother did what she did.) And while I tend to agree with scholars who say that what she was did was absolutely wrong, I defer judgment with this simple observation:

Sometimes searching for God is simply irrational.

Awareness and Practice

The beginning of wisdom is this: Get wisdom,
and whatever else you get, get insight.

—Proverbs 4:7

To live the Mystery of the People of God means that you have to look past logic and reason. Human beings are irrational; we cannot be reduced to logical algorithms that will predict how we will (or should) behave. To live this mystery means letting yourself be surprised and disappointed by the unpredictability of human behavior.

When you see someone who is behaving irrationally, instead of dismissing that person as being illogical, foolish, or unwise, ask yourself if their behavior might be reasonable in some way. Can that behavior be explained in terms of fairness? What does this person's behavior tell you about what they think is fair or unfair? What insights does this tell you about how this person sees the world? What new perspectives does this offer you?

This practice does not mean that you have to agree with or excuse another person's actions. Rather, it is meant to help broaden your perspective so that you can find God in all things, even ones that make no sense.

29

Righteousness

Elizabeth of Töss

1292–1336

Love cannot take root in the human heart unless there is hatred of the enemy, that is, of the devil and sin.

—The Blessed Virgin Mary to Elizabeth of Töss

There's a popular saying I really don't like: "Hate the sin, love the sinner."

Human beings are really bad at separating the sinner from the sin. We tend to define people by their actions; when someone sins—that is, when someone does evil—that person is defined by that evil and they become evil in our eyes. We end up hating the sinner *because* we hate the sin. And besides, once we start hating something, *anything*, hate seems to take over the heart.

So how do I make sense of the Blessed Virgin Mary's admonition to the great-niece of St. Elizabeth of Hungary (and Dominican nun), Elizabeth of Töss, that we should hate the enemy of the human race?

Perhaps I need to ponder the meaning of *hate*.

I can think of hate as an intense dislike for someone or something. In that case, hate leads to the desire to avoid the source of things that cause such loathing. (Such desire can be called *aversion*.) Aversion makes communion with others impossible because I seek to separate myself from those I hate. Truly, hate is diabolical.

I can also think of hate as the opposite of love. Since my favorite definition of *love* is "goodness giving itself away," a logical definition of *hate* seems to be "keeping goodness to one's self." That means I refuse to give others what they need to thrive. I don't like that option either.

Maybe the word I should be looking for is *righteousness*.

Now Elizabeth of Töss begins to make some sense. She is telling me that I must remain righteous in the face of evil: when faced with evil, I must keep goodness close to my heart. The devil wants to steal goodness from me. He wants to convince me that people are no good. To remain righteous in the face of those temptations (and those temptations are legion) means that I have to remember to see my own goodness, find it, treasure it, and share it with others.

If you can find God in all things, you will find goodness in all things. When you do that, there is no room for hate, only for righteousness.

Awareness and Practice

"'You shall love your neighbor and hate your enemy.' But I say to you, Love your enemies and pray for those who persecute you, so that you may be children of your Father in heaven; for he makes his sun rise on the evil and on the good, and sends rain on the righteous and on the unrighteous."

—Matthew 5:43–45

The People of God are bound together by righteousness. To live this mystery, you need to focus on people's goodness. That will require you to overlook a lot, forgive much, and forget more. If we don't let go of those imperfections, we end up planting the seeds of hate, from which grow vines that will choke the goodness of the People of God. Righteousness, however, eliminates such hate at its root.

When you think of someone as "evil" or "sinful," focus on something that is good in that person, some redeeming characteristic. If you cannot find anything specific, focus on the hope that there is some goodness in that person; perhaps they themselves have not realized it is there. Imagine how you would react to noticing that goodness in them.

Focusing on the good does not excuse a person's bad behavior; it ensures that *your* actions will be motivated by love, not anger.

30

Service

John the Evangelist

First Century

All who hate a brother or sister are murderers, and you know that murderers do not have eternal life abiding in them. We know love by this, that he laid down his life for us—and we ought to lay down our lives for one another. How does God's love abide in anyone who has the world's goods and sees a brother or sister in need and yet refuses help? Little children, let us love not in word or speech, but in truth and action.

—1 John 3:15–18

John the Evangelist has been identified by many as the beloved disciple who reclined at Jesus' side during the Last Supper (John 13:23–25), stood by the Blessed Virgin Mary at the foot of Jesus' cross (John 19:25–26), and beat Peter in a foot race to Jesus' empty tomb (John 20:2–5).

If anyone can be called a mystic, John the Evangelist can. Just read the beginning of his gospel if you don't believe me; only a mystic could write such words. He teaches all mystics an essential lesson, that of service, which he learned at the Last Supper, when Jesus washed the disciples' feet (John 13:1–20).

We find God not by simply doing good deeds (if that were the case, even atheists would find God). We find God by doing good deeds in a particular way, and that way is modeled after the lesson Jesus gave us in washing the disciples' feet.

First, it is *discerning*. Just as Jesus knew that God the Father "had given all things into his hands" (John 13:3), you have to know how to best serve others in a way that brings glory to God. We need the Holy Spirit's wisdom to discern the difference between works of mercy that serve worldly goals—even when those goals benefit others—and those that serve heavenly ones.

Second, to find God through service, we have to make ourselves *vulnerable*. Jesus did this by taking off his outer robe. Our "outer robes" are the things that we use to separate ourselves from others. Maybe our outer robe is our opinion about who is "worthy" and who isn't. Maybe it's a feeling of futility, a feeling that no matter what we do, it won't make a difference, so why bother.

Third, we have to be *committed*. Just as Jesus poured water into the washbasin, only by pouring our entire selves into the good works we do will we find God. Hold nothing back; go all in. We have no need to worry about how much we have to give because we can trust in God's incomprehensible generosity.

Finally, we have to be *gentle* in the way we perform our service to others. Anyone who has had plantar fasciitis knows how painful even the gentlest touch can be. When Jesus wiped the disciples' feet with a towel, he must have used a soft and gentle touch. Following Jesus' example, we must be careful not to put too much pressure on those whom we serve by making demands of them.

So be a person for others, but be a particular *kind* of person for others: be discerning, be vulnerable, be committed, and be gentle. That's how you will find God in service.

Awareness and Practice

"If I, your Lord and teacher, have washed your feet, you also ought to wash one another's feet. For I have set you an example, that you also should do as I have done to you."

—John 13:14–15

To experience the Mystery of the People of God, you must encounter others so you can hear their needs and learn to serve them with wisdom and compassion. But to fully experience this mystery, you must also share your needs with them so they can wash your feet.

Reflect on the good deeds that others do for you and your motivation for reciprocating them. Are you motivated by the desire to bring honor to yourself? To improve the lives of others? To bring praise and glory to God?

The truth is that probably all three reasons serve as motivation for your good deeds. The real test is in your answers to the following questions: if something you did brought great honor to yourself but it failed to bring glory to God, would you still do it? If something you could do would improve the lives of billions but fail to bring glory to God, would you still do it?

31

Liturgy

Hildegarde of Bingen

1098–1179

After this, I saw the image of a woman as large as a great city, with a wonderful crown on her head and arms from which a splendor hung like sleeves, hanging from Heaven to Earth. Her womb was pierced like a net with many openings, with a huge multitude of people running in and out. She had no legs or feet, but stood balanced on her womb in front of the altar that stands before the eyes of God, embracing it with her outstretched hands and gazing sharply with her eyes throughout all of Heaven.

—Hildegarde of Bingen

Hildegarde of Bingen, a Benedictine abbess and polymath, recorded this vision in her book *Scivias*, which is short for Scito Vias Domino (*Know the Ways of the Lord*). Hildegarde's writing was more prophetic than mystical; *Scivias* reads as if it were written by an Old Testament prophet like Jeremiah or Isaiah rather than by a mystic like Teresa of Ávila or Catherine of Siena. Hildegarde does not describe a path to divine union; rather, she called out priests and monks who were sluggish, uninspired, and lazy in their vocation. She wrote less about what the content of her visions were and more about their meaning.

For example, in the vision above, Hildegarde explains that the woman represents the Church, and the "wonderful crown on her head" represents the apostles and the martyrs. The arms represent the priests: through their ministry, God's grace reaches down from heaven through the sacraments. The woman's net-like womb with children represents the Church's "maternal kindness, which is so clever at capturing faithful souls by diverse goads of virtue, and in which the trusting peoples devoutly lead their lives by the faith of their true belief." That she had no legs or feet indicates that she is incomplete: the Church is not fully formed (and there has been plenty of evidence—recent and ancient—that supports this interpretation). The Church is, after all, a work in progress, and like any living organism, has her growing pains. The woman's embrace of the altar represents the liturgy: "This good work is in God's sight the sweetest sacrifice, at which the Church constantly labors, striving with her whole desire for heavenly things in bringing virtues to fruition."

Typically, when I think of liturgy, I think of formulas that dictate what we do in Mass. Hildegarde challenges me to think of liturgy as a place to find God. It connects us with others. The ritual actions I perform during the Mass—blessing myself with holy water; signing my forehead, lips, and chest before hearing the Gospel; and reciting the formulaic responses—all serve to break my normal patterns of behavior. (After all, seldom do I greet people with the words *Peace be with you* as I do during Mass—though that might not be a bad idea.) In breaking those patterns, my attention is reset and directed outside of myself—toward others, toward the altar, and toward Christ.

I can find God in liturgy for this simple reason: in the liturgy I am redirecting my attention toward the divine.

Awareness and Practice

While they were eating, Jesus took a loaf of bread, and after blessing it he broke it, gave it to the disciples, and said, "Take, eat; this is my body."

—Matthew 26:26

Liturgy allows us to share our experiences of the divine with others, a process that serves as the ligaments and tendons of the Body of Christ. Through liturgy, the People of God are transformed from a community of individuals into the Mystical Body of Christ.

You can live this mystery by recognizing the rituals in your life and by integrating new ones. Of course, there is the liturgy you celebrate in common as a Church. But there are also the private, more intimate liturgies of your daily life: saying "I love you" to your spouse at the end of every call, preparing a cup of tea for someone, calling a friend, walking the dogs.

Pick an activity and treat it as a ritual: make the practice deliberate, mindful, oriented toward another, and dedicated to God. No longer are these mindless habits or chores; they become powerful encounters with God in others because, for a brief moment, your attention is not on yourself but on the People of God.

And that's one way to find God in all things.

32

Reality

Thomas Aquinas

1225–1274

So it is that sacred doctrine is a science because it proceeds from principles established by the light of a higher science, namely, the science of God and the blessed. Hence, just as the musician accepts on authority the principles taught him by the mathematician, so sacred science is established on principles revealed by God.

—Thomas Aquinas

I often wonder what Catholic theology would be like today if St. Thomas Aquinas had been Chinese.

Instead of reconciling Christian revelation with Aristotelian philosophy, the Chinese Thomas might have tried to reconcile Christian revelation with the philosophy of Laozi. The Chinese Thomas might have tried to apply the principles from the *Analects* of Confucius to his understanding of how Christians ought to live. Instead of writing beautiful prayers, the Chinese Thomas might have developed meditation practices inspired by the Buddha that draw us into experiencing the presence of Christ.

But Thomas Aquinas was not Chinese; he was Italian. And while he never entered one of the many Taoist monasteries in the Wudang Mountains of China, he did enter the Dominican Order when he was seventeen. Thomas studied under St. Albert the Great, became a doctor of theology at the University of Paris by the time he was twenty-five, and spent his life learning, teaching, and writing. His best-known work, *Summa Theologiae*, is a classic in Western theology and philosophy. In the first part of the *Summa*, Thomas discusses the nature of God, the Trinity, creation, and the concepts of good and evil. In the second part (which is the longest), he discusses the nature of ethics and virtue. The third part focuses on the mysteries of Christ.

Thomas never finished the *Summa*. On December 6, 1273, while celebrating a Mass, he received a vision. After that, he stopped writing. "All that I have written," he said, "appears to be as so much straw after the things that have been revealed to me."

That doesn't mean that what he had written was worthless. Human beings are, after all, pattern-recognition machines: when our brain sees an object, it searches for memories that resemble that object. This process is called *pareidolia* and explains why I can look up into the sky and see a cloud that looks like a bunny rabbit. Thomas saw the patterns of God's revelation reflected in Aristotelian and neo-Platonic philosophy, which resulted in the *Summa*. Sometimes, however, we mistake the patterns we see for the thing itself (for example, that cloud *is* a bunny rabbit!). That will give us a distorted view of reality.

When we look for God, we are not trying to run from reality. Rather, finding God means engaging reality at its deepest level. And that engagement calls us to constantly ask questions about what we perceive in the world around us, challenge our assumptions, and imagine different possibilities, such as wondering what theology would be like if Thomas Aquinas had been Chinese.

Awareness and Practice

For God shows no partiality.

—Romans 2:11

We don't engage reality in isolation; rather, every time we engage with reality, we enter into a relationship with someone or something. When we focus on the relationships that knit reality together, we discover that barriers become an impossibility. That truth lies at the heart of the Mystery of the People of God.

You live this mystery by breaking down the barriers that separate you from others. You can do that by questioning your assumptions. Read something that challenges your long-held beliefs. (For example, you might read a book from an opposing theological perspective, or news from a source that has an opposing political bent.) That doesn't mean that your beliefs are wrong; rather, it will expand your frame of reference and give you an opportunity to share in the way other people experience reality.

This can be a challenging practice. If you feel threatened, stop. Take a deep breath and identify exactly what it is that threatens you. Then acknowledge your feelings by saying to yourself, *Yes, I am feeling threatened. It's okay to feel this way. I am loved even though I feel threatened.*

33

Harmony

Paul the Apostle

c. 4 B.C.–c. A.D. 62–64

*We do not live to ourselves, and we do not die to ourselves. If we
live, we live to the Lord, and if we die, we die to the Lord; so then,
whether we live or whether we die, we are the Lord's.*

—Romans 14:7–8

I think I am attracted to mysticism because I like to think
that I can do it alone; mysticism can be defined, after all, as
one's personal, lived experience of God. I can run off to some
solitary place—perhaps at the base of a large tree along the
snow-covered banks of a small creek—and be alone with my
thoughts about all things divine. Mysticism allows me the lux-
ury of avoiding other people, who are too often unreasonable,
unkind, uncharitable, and disappointing.

But that's not *Christian* mysticism. A Christian mystic is
someone who seeks a personal, lived experience with Jesus
Christ, that is, with another human being (who also happens
to be fully divine). I can have a lived experience with the
divine only by living it with another person: Jesus Christ. And
as Paul the apostle teaches me, Christ *is* other people.

Paul encountered Christ in the communities he persecuted. When Christ appeared to him in a vision outside Damascus and called, "Saul, Saul, why do you persecute me?" (Acts 9:4), Paul must have thought, "I'm not persecuting you. I'm persecuting the people who believe you are the Messiah."

Christ, in essence, replied, "And you think there's a difference?"

Paul could not see that the people he persecuted were the Body of Christ. When he learned that lesson, he worked to maintain the unity of that body. Paul didn't encounter Christ in the Gospels—they hadn't been written yet. He encountered Christ in the communities of Christians he persecuted. And by encountering Christ through community, Paul learned a basic lesson about finding God: we find God in the harmony that exists among people. Yes, we are distinct, and these distinctions have very real ramifications on the way we live. But these distinctions do not make us different, for we are all one body through baptism in Jesus Christ.

Harmony requires that we give people the space to discover what God is calling them to do, and then letting them share that with others. The pursuit of God is really the pursuit of unity and harmony. And we do that not by pursuing what is good for ourselves, but by pursuing the good of others.

Awareness and Practice

"I give you a new commandment, that you love one another. Just as I have loved you, you also should love one another. By this everyone will know that you are my disciples, if you have love for one another."

—John 13:34–35

The mystery of baptism teaches us to seek unity and harmony in our communities. We discover unity and harmony by working together toward a common purpose. This brings us ever deeper into the mystery of community, where we find God in our collaboration.

Ask yourself, "What does harmony look like?" How do you collaborate with others? Spend time gazing at those examples without analyzing, dissecting, or manipulating them. What qualities does that harmony reflect in the world? Do you see this harmony reflected in yourself and others?

Now imagine what your communities—your families, workplaces, schools, neighborhoods, and the world—would look like if they reflected that harmony. Can you imagine bringing some of that harmony into your life? What do you need to change in yourself to make that vision a reality? Ask God for the grace to make those changes.

34

Forgiveness

Helen Prejean

b. 1939

Now, somewhat awakened, I look back in amazement at how ignorant I was. But I guess when you're not awake, you're not awake. Waking up to the suffering of people who are different from us is a long process, and has a whole lot to do with what community we belong to and whose consciousness and life experiences impact our own on a daily basis. I have a hunch I'm going to be waking up till the moment I die.

—Helen Prejean

I'm not sure I would say I have heroes.

I am, however, inspired by people who have helped me go beyond myself and do something to correct injustice. Sister Helen Prejean is one of them. She is best known for her activism against the death penalty; she authored the book *Dead Man Walking* (which was later made into a movie and an opera).

I volunteered with the National Coalition to Abolish the Death Penalty when it worked toward repeal in Connecticut, Illinois, and Kansas. (We were successful in Connecticut and

Illinois but not in Kansas.) I didn't do much—I wrote letters and made phone calls. The latter was a real challenge for me because I have an irrational fear of calling people on the phone, especially people I don't know. It sometimes triggers a mild panic attack.

When the opera based on Sister Helen's book came to the Lyric Opera for its Chicago premiere, my dad, who's a season ticket holder, invited me to attend a talk she was going to give. I jumped at the chance.

Sister Helen explained that *Dead Man Walking* wasn't about the death penalty. It was about what we do as a society with our hurt. It was about the families who struggled with the ideas of forgiveness and vengeance in the most heart-wrenching of circumstances. The question that Sister Helen left me thinking about after the talk was bigger than whether we should abolish the death penalty (and, to be clear, we must). I was left asking myself whether our society believes in vengeance or forgiveness. "Would we rather get even," I remember Sister Helen asking the crowd at one point, "or do we try to become whole?"

I know that I would like to become whole, and that requires me to walk the path of forgiveness. That's easier said than done, because forgiveness is fraught with tension. On the one hand, to forgive someone, I choose not to hold whatever wrong they did against them. On the other hand, I cannot excuse them of that wrongdoing—what that person did was wrong, and they are culpable.

I don't know how to manage that tension, but I trust that God can. Maybe that's where I find God—in that tension. And in doing so, God can teach me how to forgive myself for the times when I would rather get even.

Awareness and Practice

"For if you forgive others their trespasses, your heavenly Father will also forgive you; but if you do not forgive others, neither will your Father forgive your trespasses."

—Matthew 6:14–15

The Mystery of the People of God is the mystery of forgiveness. You cannot live this mystery when you are motivated by vengeance—when you think that because someone hit you first, you are entitled to hit back harder. Without forgiveness, the Body of Christ would tear itself apart.

I cannot tell you that you have to forgive those who have wronged you—forgiveness must be given freely (that's why Jesus was able to forgive those who crucified him: he was completely free in doing his Father's will). What I can do is invite you to consider your feelings toward someone who has wronged you. If you feel bitterness, anger, pain, or fear, do you desire to feel something else? If so, imagine what those feelings might be. How do you react to that possibility? Ask God for the grace to make sense of it all.

If you notice that you feel something other than bitterness, anger, pain, or fear, ask yourself if forgiveness is possible, and then ask God to show you what that might look like.

35

Justice

Moses

Fourteenth–Thirteenth Century B.C.

Moses said to the LORD, "See, you have said to me, 'Bring up this people'; but you have not let me know whom you will send with me. Yet you have said, 'I know you by name, and you have also found favor in my sight.' Now if I have found favor in your sight, show me your ways, so that I may know you and find favor in your sight. Consider too that this nation is your people."

—Exodus 33:12–13

A friend of mine once laid into me about politics. "The problem with you *Demon*crats," he said with an oh-so-clever grin, "is that you don't believe in God." (Maybe he never read my book *Little Lessons from the Saints*.)

"Well," I said in my defense, "I'm not really a Democrat; I'm more of an anarcho-syndicalist." (Anarcho-syndicalism is a model of economic organization in which free and equal individuals voluntarily work together to meet the economic needs of all.) Not sure how to respond, he simply laughed, and our brewing argument quickly ended.

Not that I don't find politics interesting. I do. I *love* politics. I am fascinated with the way different groups answer the basic question of how to order a just society. The question about justice is what leads me to believe that I can find God in politics.

Well, that and Moses.

Moses teaches me that the result of finding God is the pursuit of justice. Moses found God in the burning bush, and that encounter led him to become a revolutionary. God called Moses to lead the Israelites out of Egypt, to overthrow the established and unjust political system that was oppressing his people. He also established a new political order. Through a mystical experience on Mt. Sinai, God gave Moses the Ten Commandments that established how the Israelites were to live with God and with one another.

We need to imitate Moses if we want to live in a world of justice and peace, a world that can come only from God. We have to respond to an encounter with God with revolutionary acts of justice. We need to confront the Pharaohs of our day—we need to stand up to the forces of oppression. We need to lead ourselves from the slavery of our attachments to money, power, and status toward the freedom that allows us to submit to God's will. We need to be patient like Moses, because finding God can feel like wandering in the desert for forty long years, learning to accept that meaningful changes take time. Finally, we have to be able to have an imagination like that of Moses, committed to the vision of a land that flows with milk and honey, a land that flows with justice and peace.

Perhaps that is why there is so much injustice in the world: we've limited our search for God to safe places we call "religious," "sacred," or "holy."

Awareness and Practice

For the word of the LORD is upright,
  and all his work is done in faithfulness.
He loves righteousness and justice;
  the earth is full of the steadfast love of the LORD.

—Psalm 33:4–5

To live the Mystery of the People of God is to respond to the call to live in communion with others and with creation. It is a communion based on justice, on intimate relationships with God and others. When we correct injustice, we restore our right relationships with others, and through those relationships, we enter into a right relationship with God. Through this communion, we experience God. When we don't live this mystery, communion remains out of reach, and the violence of injustice is the inevitable result.

Where do you see injustice? Where do you see needs that are unmet and responsibilities that go unfulfilled? Listen to the voices of those who are crying out for justice, and ask yourself, "Am I helping those who are oppressed meet their needs? Or am I contributing to people not living up to their responsibilities toward one another?"

These can be difficult questions to ponder, especially if you feel that you or your group is being attacked. Ask God for the freedom to see beyond allegiances you may have and the grace to hear the cries of those who are oppressed with an open heart. Also ask for the grace not to demonize those who deny justice. Rather, ask God to show you how you might act with compassion toward them.

Finally, listen to God to show you what to do to correct the injustice you see. In the pursuit of justice, no act is too small or insignificant.

36

Reconciliation

Jacob

Second Millennium B.C.

"No, please; if I find favor with you, then accept my present from my hand; for truly to see your face is like seeing the face of God—since you have received me with such favor. Please accept my gift that is brought to you, because God has dealt graciously with me, and because I have everything I want."

—Genesis 33:10–11

When I think of mysticism, I often think of dreams in which God is giving me some message that I can share with the world. That's what happened to the Old Testament patriarch Jacob: he dreamed of angels ascending and descending a ladder that connected heaven and earth (see Genesis 28:10–22). The Lord himself promised in this dream that Jacob's descendants would inherit the land on which Jacob stood. Jacob responded, "Surely the LORD is in this place—and I did not know it!" (Genesis 28:16) and erected a stone pillar commemorating the place, which he named Bethel, "the House of God."

I also imagine mystics have angelic visions. Jacob saw angels, though he ended up getting into a fight with one (see Genesis 32:22–32). While Jacob won that fight, the angel broke his hip (leaving Jacob with a limp the rest of his life). Jacob did manage to get a blessing from the angel before the fight was over: "You shall no longer be called Jacob, but Israel, for you have striven with God and with humans, and have prevailed" (Genesis 32:28).

"I have seen God face to face, and yet my life is preserved," Jacob said after receiving the angel's blessing (Genesis 32:30). No one said mysticism would be easy.

I don't think I've ever considered an encounter with my older brother as something mystical. Sure, my conversations with him are pleasant enough, sometimes frustrating (he is my older brother, after all), but I have never confused him with an angel.

Jacob, on the other hand, did.

Jacob had tricked his older brother, Esau, out of his inheritance (Genesis 25:29–34), and he tricked his father, Isaac, into giving him the blessing of the firstborn, which rightfully belonged to Esau (Genesis 27). Fearing Esau's wrath, Jacob fled to the land of his uncle Laban. After many years, Jacob returned to make peace with his brother. As he approached

Esau, Jacob feared for his life. But Esau ran to Jacob and embraced him (Genesis 33:4).

"Truly to see your face," Jacob addressed his brother through tears of joy "is like seeing the face of God—since you have received me with such favor" (Genesis 33:10).

Now *that* is a mystical experience. The story of Jacob reminds me that I can see the face of God in others. Perhaps that is what makes us the People of God: to see God in the face of another is to recognize a family resemblance and see that we are all sisters and brothers.

Awareness and Practice

"Be merciful, just as your Father is merciful."

—Luke 6:36

You can live the Mystery of the People of God by reconciling with others. Reconciliation builds upon forgiveness; it is a conscious decision to rebuild a relationship. Reconciliation requires contrition (saying "I'm sorry" rather than "Can you forgive me?"). Reconciliation seeks to restore harmony, and it is the aim of justice.

Consider relationships you have that are injured. Among them may be a relationship with another person; perhaps one might be a relationship you have with an organization (such as the Church); another may be a relationship you have with your environment. Which step—contrition, forgiveness, harmony, or justice—do you feel is necessary to restore that relationship? Imagine taking that step and being reconciled with whomever (or whatever). Ask God for the grace to begin contemplating such a reconciliation.

37

Kinship

Nicholas Black Elk

1863–1950

*And while I stood there I saw more than I can tell and I
understood more than I saw; for I was seeing in a sacred manner
the shapes of all things in the spirit, and the shape of all shapes as
they must live together like one being. And I saw that the sacred
hoop of my people was one of many hoops that made one circle,
wide as daylight and as starlight, and in the center grew one
mighty flowering tree to shelter all the children of one mother and
one father. And I saw that it was holy.*

—Black Elk

In the 1985 sci-fi film *Enemy Mine*, humanity waged an interstellar war with a race of reptilian humanoids known as the Drac. At one point in the movie, a human soldier named Willis Davidge (played by Dennis Quaid) and a Drac soldier named Jeriba "Jerry" Shigan (played by Louis Gossett Jr.) share a moment where they found God. Davidge reads a line from the Drac sacred text: "If one receives evil from another, let one not do evil in return. Rather, let him extend love to the enemy, that love might unite them."

"I've heard this all before," Davidge says, quizzically.

"Of course you have," Jeriba replies. "Truth is truth."

That's the thing about finding God: when you find God, you find truth, regardless of the cultural source from where that truth came. Indeed, to find God, you need to learn a common language, a kind of lingua franca that allows you to share experiences of the divine.

The Oglala Lakota holy man Nicholas Black Elk spoke that language fluently. Black Elk came of age during the Black Hills Wars (1876–1877); he fought at the Battle of the Little Big Horn with Crazy Horse, his second cousin. He traveled throughout the United States and Europe as part of Buffalo Bill Cody's Wild West Show. Black Elk converted to Catholicism as an adult and became a catechist and preacher. He is credited with bringing over four hundred people into the Catholic faith. Yet he is best known for the enduring vision he narrated to the poet John Neihardt in the religious classic *Black Elk Speaks*—the noted Lakota author and activist Vine Deloria Jr. noted that *Black Elk Speaks* had "become a North American bible of all tribes." What makes Black Elk's vision enduring are not its details or possible meanings—mystical visions are complex, and the complexity of Black Elk's vision is magnified by the relationship he had with Neihardt, who had rewritten some of Black Elk's stories. The enduring vision of Nicholas Black Elk was his ability to live in two worlds.

Among the Lakota who continue to follow the traditional ways—including many in his own family—Black Elk was, and continues to be, a traditional Oglala holy man. Among Catholics—Native and non-Native alike—Black Elk is a model of Christian discipleship. Black Elk belonged to both of these worlds because he belonged to neither: he belonged to a world that mystics call home, where everyone, and everything, belongs.

Awareness and Practice

Let them praise the name of the LORD,
for his name alone is exalted;
his glory is above earth and heaven.

—Psalm 148:13

The identity of the People of God is not limited to those who share creeds, traditions, or tribal histories. Rather, the People of God includes everyone and everything, since they all share in God's being. We are, in a sense, one family, and we speak one language. To live the Mystery of the People of God requires that we learn our family language.

Spend time learning the language of nature. Listen to the birds, the trees, the rocks, the land, the water, and the sky. What do they say to you? How do they praise God? What sounds that you hear now sound similar to what you have heard before? What new words do you learn? How might you share their voices with others?

Apply the skills you've learned from listening to nature to listening to other people. How do you approach them differently? What new words do you learn? How might you give voice to their words?

38

Interspirituality

Wayne Teasdale

1945–2004

Interspirituality is open to growth in perspective; it implies a commitment to always push forward toward a more adequate understanding of the source, the meaning of life, and the best methods of proceeding in our spiritual lives.

—Wayne Teasdale

When I was going through my formation in the Secular Franciscan Order, a friar said to me, "If you want to know what Franciscan spirituality is all about, contemplate this image." He then handed me a picture of Pope John Paul II standing with leaders of the world's religions in front of the *Portiuncula*, the home of the Franciscan family.

Being a Franciscan—that is, living the gospel after the manner and example of St. Francis of Assisi—calls me to recognize and respect the divine seed that is in the heart of every human being. Regardless of our religious background, each one of us is on some sort of spiritual journey, and I can learn from the experiences of others. (Who knows, maybe they can even learn something from me!) My calling is to practice *interspirituality*.

Wayne Teasdale was a Catholic monk who has helped me understand what that call means.

He was a professor at DePaul University in Chicago and the Chicago Catholic Theological Union, and he spent much of his life finding common ground among the world's religions. Interspirituality, he explained in his book *The Mystic Heart*, is the sharing of experiences across religious traditions. Interspirituality invites me, as a Catholic, to share my experiences with people of other religions, and invites people of other religions to share their experiences with me. Interspirituality is not about eliminating our differences—it is about appreciating and learning from one another so that we can all grow in wisdom.

Brother Wayne explains the meaning of interspirituality using the parable of several blind people touching an elephant. Each person is asked to describe the elephant. The first person touches the trunk and says the elephant is solid and wide. The second person touches the elephant's tail and says the elephant is thin and spindly. A third person touches the elephant's ears and says the elephant is flat and floppy. The fourth touches the elephant's side and says it is a rough, nondescript creature. Each person knows one aspect of the elephant; each person describes the elephant in a way that is true and valid from that person's perspective. So it is with religion.

The spiritual journey travels a path that shows us new perspectives. While we may never leave our path—our tradition—we may intersect with people on different paths. Such intersections are where we will find God.

Awareness and Practice

He is the image of the invisible God, the firstborn of all creation; for in him all things in heaven and on earth were created, things visible and invisible, whether thrones or dominions or rulers or powers—all things have been created through him and for him.

—Colossians 1:15–16

As People of God, we are not defined solely by creed or doctrine; rather, we are defined by the mystery of the divine seed that is implanted in all people. To live this mystery, we must recognize that seed in others, tend to it, and nourish it.

Take time to learn the wisdom from another tradition. Here are three ways.

- Learn about another religion. How is it different? How is it the same? In what way does your understanding of God change by knowing this contrasting perspective?

- Pray with people who are of a different religion. Share your experiences of God with them and allow them to share their experiences with you.

- Serve with people from a different religion. Find a common cause or task that you can work toward with them. What do you share? What do you learn from one another?

Part Four

The Most Holy Trinity

How can I *be* with myself? How can I *be* with others? How can I *be* with God? How can I just *be*?

That is the question the mystics in this section try to answer. Of course, they don't really give me answers. Instead, they just point me toward the most important mystery of the Christian faith: the Mystery of the Most Holy Trinity.

I suspect that this mystery is really the mystery of *being* itself. To find God in all things, I will have to learn how to just be. That may be frustrating, confusing, and futile. The secret that these mystics uncover is that God is present with you in your frustration, confusion, and futility, for no other reason than that you simply *are*. I hope their stories will help you find God and stillness in simply *being*.

39

Pathways

Elisabeth of Schönau

1129–1165

On all the paths of truth, God is contemplated.
—Elisabeth of Schönau

In 1996, NASA launched the Mars Pathfinder. When the probe entered the Martian atmosphere, parachutes slowed its descent, and airbags deployed as it approached the surface, cushioning the impact. The rover—which was named after Sojourner Truth—rolled off the lander. By the time the last transmission from Pathfinder was received in 1997, NASA had collected over 2.3 billion bits of information, including evidence of water (and possibly life) on our nearest celestial neighbor.

I like to think of the Benedictine nun Elisabeth of Schönau as a spiritual Pathfinder. Her visions, which were recorded by her brother Eckebert (who served as her secretary), give us data about the divine, data that helps us discover eternal life, the Christ-within-us.

While Elisabeth is not as well-known as her contemporary Hildegarde of Bingen (with whom Elisabeth corresponded), she was just as great a mystic. Elisabeth's visions were grounded in the Church's liturgical celebrations. The *Book of the Ways to God*, for example, was revealed to her beginning on the Feast of Pentecost in 1156. Elisabeth received a series of visions in which an angel points out ten pathways to God.

- On the Path of Contemplation, you meditate on God's "marvelous essence."

- On the Path of the Active Life, you work "with a good and simple heart without murmuring and idle talk."

- On the Path of Martyrdom, you must love God more than your own life.

- On the Path of Marriage, you share your soul with your spouse.

- On the Path of Chastity, you imitate all of Christ's virtues.

- On the Path of Prelates, you embrace a life of humility and service.

- On the Path of Widows, you "seize peace of mind and the spiritual delights God offers."

- On the Path of Hermits, you practice discretion in all things.

- On the Path of Adolescents, you learn restraint.

- On the Path of Young Children, you learn good habits.

As I read about all the paths that lead to God, I realized that you're not always on the same path throughout your life, and sometimes you might have one foot in one path and one foot in another. The more I think about it, it really doesn't matter what path you are on because God *is* the path.

Awareness and Practice

A voice cries out:
In the wilderness prepare the way of the LORD,
*   make straight in the desert a highway for our God.*

—Isaiah 40:3

One way to think of the Mystery of the Most Holy Trinity is to think about it in terms of the spiritual journey: God the Father is the destination, God the Son is our companion, and God the Holy Spirit is the guide. The Father is always calling out to the Son, the Son is always walking toward the Father, and the Spirit is always drawing the two together.

In living this mystery, it is important to factor in your own spiritual journey. How would you describe your journey? What "spiritual topography"—dark valleys, lofty mountaintops, arid deserts, or verdant fields—have you traversed? Who has walked with you on this journey? What have you used as a compass? Were your footsteps heavy? Were they light? What did you carry with you along this journey? What did you leave behind?

Continue to pay attention to the path you are on. You may recognize that it is similar to one described by Elisabeth of Schönau, or maybe the Holy Spirit has led you along a new path. As you walk this path, look for God in each step.

40

Milestones

Gertrude the Great

1256–1302

"Behold, my beloved Lord! Not only my inmost soul, but every part of my body is moved toward thee!"

—Gertrude the Great

In the TV show *Preacher*, God has gone missing. A preacher named Jesse Custer, his ex-girlfriend Tulip O'Hare (who was also Jesse's partner-in-crime before he became a man of God), and their friend Proinsias Cassidy (who happens to be an Irish vampire), go searching for God. (Spoiler alert: They find God in New Orleans.)

Of course, finding God is not an adventure where I have to fight angels, demons, and a secret, pseudo-religious organization known as The Grail that controls the world. But, like Jesse and his gang, I have to ask: *Where do I even begin?*

Fortunately, St. Gertrude the Great offers me guidance. This Benedictine nun, who was taught by another great mystic, Mechtild of Magdeburg, was one of the greatest mystics of the thirteenth century. Her mysticism sprung from her devotion to Jesus' Sacred Heart; she also saw herself as a bride wedded to Christ (often referred to as "nuptial mysticism").

Gertrude also provides a road map for the soul looking for God.

The first milestone on this road map is offering praise and blessings to God on "the sacred couch of contemplation." If I want to find God, I have to take time to be present to God. I have to go beyond offering God only my words, actions, or thoughts. I have to offer God my entire being.

The second milestone on the road map to God is to offer gratitude for the gifts God has given to all creatures. I know about the power of gratitude. At the end of the day, I always thank God for the gifts I have received. Gertrude is talking about something else. She is asking me to give thanks for the gifts *others* have received. That's hard because, more often than not, I resent people for receiving a gift that I wish I had, and I end up envious.

The third milestone on the road map is divine justice. Gertrude isn't talking about God smiting evildoers. Rather, she means that the gifts I have received from God are given out of God's love and generosity, not because of anything I have done to earn them. This will leave me feeling more than a little inadequate—I can't do anything to make God love me.

God loves me unconditionally. I can't earn God's love, and I can't lose it either.

The last milestone is confidence in God's mercy. God doesn't care about my inadequacies. God doesn't use a measuring stick to compare me with others. We are all inadequate, and that's more than okay because God's own self will more than make up the difference.

Therein lies the secret genius in Gertrude's road map: her map doesn't lead me to God; it helps me realize that God is coming to me.

Awareness and Practice

Seek the LORD and his strength,
*   seek his presence continually.*

—1 Chronicles 16:11

Each Person of the Holy Trinity constantly seeks the other and finds another. God the Son, in seeking God the Father, finds God the Holy Spirit. Perhaps that is the way to think of the meaning of the word *presence*: it is the constant seeking and finding of the other. We live the Mystery of the Trinity by seeking God. And we find God in that seeking.

Follow Gertrude's road map for seeking God. Spend time each day in silent contemplation. Praise God and be present to him. Give thanks not only for the gifts you have received but also for the gifts others have received. These gifts are a result of God's magnanimity, not your merit; take time to acknowledge your inadequacy before God, and recognize that God loves you anyway.

How do you recognize God's presence as you follow this map?

41

Epiphany

Anne Catherine Emmerich

1784–1824

Oh, how touching is the good temper and childlike simplicity of these beloved kings! They give to those who come to them a share of all they have; they even hold the golden vessels to their lips and let them drink out of them, like children.

—Anne Catherine Emmerich

The Feast of the Epiphany has always been one of my favorite celebrations. Perhaps it's because I once played one of the three Magi in a Nativity play in Sunday school. My acting career peaked when I played the hindquarters of a horse in a production for the Elmhurst Children's Theater (a role that I continue to play, so I am told, to perfection).

Maybe it's because the Epiphany reaffirms that the Word of God is written in the book of nature: it was, after all, a star that led the wise men to find Jesus. Maybe it's because the Epiphany celebrates the fact that God is not the possession of any particular group of people: whoever you are, wherever you come from, God calls you to God's own self. Tribes, nations, faiths, creeds, genders—none of these things matter to God.

The German Augustinian nun Anne Catherine Emmerich recounted a detailed vision she had about the Epiphany in her book *The Life of the Blessed Virgin Mary*. In this vision, Anne gives the names of the Magi as Mensor, Sair, and Theokeno.

Now, tradition identifies the names of the Magi as Caspar, Melchior, and Balthazar. Anne explained the discrepancy:

> They were called this because it goes with their character, for these names mean: 1) He goes with love; 2) He wanders about, he approaches gently and with ingratiating manners; 3) He makes rapid decisions, he quickly directs his will to the will of God.

I think that the meanings of these names are great descriptions of each Person of the Holy Trinity: God the Father is the one who goes with love; God the Son is the one who wanders, approaching others with meekness; and God the Spirit is the one who quickly directs her will to that of God the Father and guides the steps of God the Son.

Come to think of it, those are great descriptions of how to find God: go with love, go with gentleness, and go quickly.

Awareness and Practice

When they saw that the star had stopped, they were overwhelmed with joy.

—Matthew 2:10

In the Epiphany we recognize Jesus' true identity as God the Son. That is, the Epiphany (along with the baptism of Jesus and the miracle at the wedding in Cana) introduces us to the Second Person of the Holy Trinity. And the nature of the Mystery of the Most Holy Trinity is that when you meet one of the Three Persons, you meet them all.

You can live the Mystery of the Most Holy Trinity by imitating the Magi. Meditate on the gifts they brought to the Christ child.

- **Gold:** What do you truly treasure? How do these things help you love, serve, and praise God?

- **Frankincense:** What lifts your heart? What fills you with love, mercy, and compassion?

- **Myrrh:** How do you accept your own mortality? With trepidation and unease? With a sense of peace and joy?

42

Silence

Henri Nouwen

1932–1996

A word with power is a word that comes out of silence. A word that bears fruit is a word that emerges from the silence and returns to it.

—Henri Nouwen

I have never won an argument on Facebook.

I'm not alone. In fact, I have never seen *anyone* win an argument on Facebook. The only thing I've ever seen happen is the hardening of hearts. I know this from experience. When I think about all the stupid words I've posted—whether I'm stating my own opinion or responding to another's—I'm convinced the world would have been better served had I remained silent.

"Silence," wrote one of the world's greatest spiritual teachers, Henri Nouwen, "is the home of the word." The Dutch priest and former professor at Harvard, Yale, and Notre Dame goes on to explain in his 1981 book *The Way of the Heart* that whatever power words have, that power comes from silence: "Words are meant to disclose the mystery of the silence from which they come." No wonder my words were impotent: they didn't come from silence; they came from the noisiness in my head.

Henri teaches me three lessons about the importance of silence. First, silence is a pilgrimage from the affairs of this world to the promise of the future world. For example, whenever I post something on Facebook, I'm getting involved in the affairs of this world. That's not necessarily bad—after all, if I want to be compassionate, I need to tend to the needs of people in the world. The problem is that my knowledge about the world is woefully incomplete, so my words reveal my ignorance. Silence, on the other hand, invites me to contemplate a better world, the world God imagines.

Second, silence guards the fire of the Holy Spirit within me. Henri uses an analogy to explain what he means: the mouth is like a door to a steam bath. If it's open, all the heat escapes. It is better to keep it shut.

Third, silence teaches me *how* to speak. When I speak from a place of sacred silence, I imitate God, who out of the eternal silence, spoke the Eternal Word. Silence is the only way we will learn how to speak to the needs of others.

Finding God is done in silence. I can't do it when my life is filled with the noisy nonsense of my opinions and ideas.

Awareness and Practice

Where words are many, transgression is not lacking,
  but the prudent are restrained in speech.

—Proverbs 10:19

God the Father spoke the Eternal Word—God the Son. The words of God the Son always point back to God the Father. God the Spirit is the breath behind their words. Their words are interconnected, interdependent, and intertwined, yet unique at the same time.

We can live their mystery—the Mystery of the Holy Trinity—by practicing silence in our daily life. Such silence is not necessarily a lack of words; rather, it is, in the words of Henri Nouwen, "a quality of the heart that leads to ever-growing charity."

You can practice this silence in three ways:

First, make time for silence. Choose a regular time of day when you do not speak, text, send e-mails, read, or listen to or watch media.

Second, hold your tongue. Instead of sharing your opinions about this, that, or some other thing, keep quiet. This will allow other people to speak more, which will help you understand and recognize their needs.

Finally, still your heart. When you feel that you are harboring strong emotions toward someone—whether positive or negative—sit back and practice charity toward them by praying for their well-being, health, and happiness.

43

Morality

Amma Syncletica

Fourth Century

Whatever people say by the grace of the Spirit, therefore, that is useful springs from love and ends in it.
—The Life of Syncletica

On October 11, 2019, William Barr, the attorney general of the United States, gave a speech at the University of Notre Dame. I was really bothered by something he said:

> Christianity teaches a micro-morality. We transform the world by focusing on our own personal morality and transformation.

Here's what troubles me: Jesus was not an ethical teacher, and Christianity is not a moral philosophy. Christianity is less about proper behavior than it is about trusting completely in God's will.

But instead of a "micro-morality," does Christianity teach a mystical morality? To help me ponder that question, I turned to Amma (Mother) Syncletica—one of the early Christian monastics who lived in the Egyptian desert during the fourth century—. She taught that virtuous living (i.e., morality) is meant to prepare us to contemplate the Holy Trinity. There are four virtues that Amma Syncletica thought vital:

- **Love:** "Salvation, then, is exactly this—the two-fold love of God and of our neighbour."

- **Vigilance:** "At all times, therefore, there is a need for vigilance, for he [the devil] wages war through external acts and wins victories through internal thoughts."

- **Voluntary poverty:** "The Enemy, moreover, is more soundly vanquished in the case of those who live without possessions; for he lacks the means to do harm, since the majority of our griefs and trials originate in the removal of possessions."

- **Humility:** "But so great a virtue is humility that, although the Devil seems to mimic all virtues, he does not begin to understand the nature of this one."

Our actions are not moral because they conform to a prescribed list of rules or laws of behavior. Our actions are moral because they flow from love of God and neighbor and lead to a greater love of God and neighbor. Moral living, then, allows us to find God in all things because we see through the eyes of understanding and love; we are no longer blinded by pride, anger, lust, greed, gluttony, sloth, and envy.

Awareness and Practice

He shall eat curds and honey by the time he knows how to refuse the evil and choose the good.

—Isaiah 7:15

Each Person of the Holy Trinity is a moral agent—that is, God the Father, God the Son, and God the Holy Spirit each know what is good and right; each has the freedom to choose the good and the right, and each perfectly accomplishes the good and the right. The choices and actions of each Person of the Trinity flow from love and lead to greater love. When we act morally—when we act out of love in a way that leads to greater love—we participate in that mystery.

Try practicing the virtues described by Amma Syncletica. As you practice these virtues, notice where you sense God's presence.

- **Love:** Act with generosity and kindness toward God, others, and yourself.

- **Vigilance:** Carefully watch the thoughts and feelings behind your words and actions. Where do they come from? Is it a place of love? Where do they lead? Is that a place of greater love?

- **Voluntary poverty:** Pick one thing in your life that you value, that you think brings you happiness. Imagine what your life would be like without it. Where do you find happiness then? If possible, give that thing away.

- **Humility:** Listen to others with respect. Value their presence. Express gratitude for whatever it is they share with you, regardless of whether it is pleasant or unpleasant.

44

Joy

Bridget of Sweden

1303–1373

The Father's joy is that of the Son and the Holy Spirit: the Son's joy is that of the Father and the Spirit: and the Holy Spirit's joy is that of the Father and the Son.

—Bridget of Sweden

Happiness is part of our national creed. "We hold these truths to be self-evident," begins the Declaration of Independence, "that all men are created equal, that they are endowed by their Creator with certain unalienable Rights, that among these are Life, Liberty and the pursuit of Happiness."

The thing is, we're not very good at pursuing happiness. Despite our national obsession with happiness, it continues to elude us. Perhaps that's because we don't know what happiness is. "The goal is so elusive and hard to define, it's impossible to pinpoint when it's even been reached—a recipe for anxiety," concludes Ruth Whippman in her book *America the Anxious: How Our Pursuit of Happiness Is Creating a Nation of Nervous Wrecks*. The more we're told to value happiness—and a lot of people have made a lot of money selling books that tell you how to be happy—the less happy we become (a hypothesis confirmed by researchers at the University of California, Berkeley). We've become so fixated on being happy that we've forgotten how to exist without happiness.

The problem is that we're pursuing happiness as if it were another commodity to be consumed. Instead, we should be pursuing *joy*. To understand what joy is, Bridget of Sweden tells me to look to the Holy Trinity. In Bridget's book *Prophecies and Revelations*, which is a masterpiece of medieval Swedish literature, she shares a sermon she heard from an angel. The divine joy the angel described to Bridget stemmed from God's love:

> The divine wisdom of God willed all things to be what they are for his own honor and glory. He had no need of them; it was not to make up for any deficiency in himself—something wanting to his goodness or joy—there can be no defect or deficiency in God. It was his love, and his love alone, which led him to create; that there might be beings, apart from himself, whose existence should be an existence of joy, deriving from his own being and joy.

We don't need to find God by chasing happiness; we find God by living joyfully.

Awareness and Practice

*"I have said these things to you so that my joy may be in you,
and that your joy may be complete."*

—John 15:11

The Father rejoiced in the Son and the Holy Spirit; the Son rejoiced in the Father and the Holy Spirit; the Holy Spirit rejoiced in the Father and the Son. Their joy was so complete that they were one. Joy can be a key to unlock the Mystery of the Holy Trinity. Whenever we share another person's joy, we imitate the behavior of the Father, Son, and Holy Spirit. To live the Mystery of the Holy Trinity means living a life of true and perfect joy with others.

You can live true and perfect joy by rejoicing in the blessings other people receive. When a good thing happens to someone else, rejoice for them (even when that person is someone you might call an "enemy"). The flip side is to share another person's sorrows while never losing trust in God's ultimate goodness. When someone is sad, be sad with them.

This will be a challenging practice if you tend to get angry at another person's blessing or success or if you find pleasure in the misfortune and failures of others. Such attitudes will make living this mystery—or any mystery—impossible.

45

Attention

Peter of Alcántara

1499–1562

The work of meditation is to consider with attentive study the things of God, now busy on one, now on another, in order to move our hearts to some appropriate affections of the will—striking the flint to secure a spark.

—Peter of Alcántara

There is good reason for why we should listen to Peter of Alcántara when it comes to the topic of meditation and prayer: the Franciscan friar was the spiritual director to one of Christianity's greatest mystics, St. Teresa of Ávila.

Meditation and prayer, Peter explains, "engender that affection and sentiment in the will which we call devotion, and this incites and urges us on to well-doing." The purpose of meditation and prayer, according to Peter, is to engender devotion: the promptness and readiness to undertake all that is good.

I'm somewhat put off by the word *meditation*. (It seems so bougie these days.) Maybe a better word would be "attention." That is, to meditate on God is simply to pay attention to God.

Peter offers tips on how we can pay attention to God in his handbook *Treatise on Prayer and Meditation*.

His first counsel is to always remember that our purpose is devotion. We should not prefer one method of meditation (for example, *lectio divina*, the daily *examen*, or centering prayer) to any other; we should prefer only those methods that help us grow in devotion. (This can be tricky, since the prayers we often choose are the ones that make us feel good or holy, not because they lead us closer to God; Peter calls this a kind of "spiritual greed.")

Peter also explains that to pay attention to God is not the same as doing theological, philosophical, or etymological research and analysis. Rather, when we pay attention to God, we engage "the speculative intellect," that is, our imagination. However, we need to be disciplined when using our imagination so that we don't follow a rabbit down a hole of fantasies.

Sometimes we might have strong feelings that can be distracting. For example, if we are paying attention to the Crucifixion, we may be overcome with feelings of loss and sorrow. Peter advises us not to force any particular emotions but "to receive such affections as His mercy shall give . . . let him not be cast down when none are given." If we experience affections during meditation, we should pause and take time to savor them, for they are a grace. And sometimes, we might not feel anything. That, too, Peter counsels, is also a grace.

Maybe the biggest challenge to finding God in all things is that we just don't pay attention. But I'm hopeful that Peter of Alcántara's advice will help me learn how to be more attentive to God. It would, after all, be a real shame if I missed God simply because I was distracted for a moment.

Awareness and Practice

Be still, and know that I am God!
I am exalted among the nations,
I am exalted in the earth.

—Psalm 46:10

Meditation is often seen as something passive—one just sits and is still. But that stillness is not inactive. The mind races from one thought to another. The body aches and itches. Sound and noise intrude into your sacred space. Meditation can be torturous, a kind of holy hell. When you can respond with patience, gentleness, and love to distractions that torment your meditation, you will begin to imitate the patience of God the Father, the gentleness of God the Son, and the love of God the Holy Spirit.

*

Evaluate your meditation practice. How has your practice helped you grow in patience? How has it helped you grow in gentleness? How has it helped you grow in love of God, others (especially those you might consider unlovable), and yourself?

If, on the other hand, you do not see yourself reflect the patience of God the Father, the gentleness of God the Son, or the love of God the Holy Spirit, perhaps it's time to change your practice. A spiritual director can help you find new ways to do that.

46

Presence

Brother Lawrence of the Resurrection

1614–1691

*The holiest, most ordinary, and most necessary practice of the
spiritual life is that of the presence of God. It is to take delight in
and become accustomed to his divine company, speaking humbly
and conversing lovingly with him all the time, at every moment,
without rule or measure, especially in times of temptation,
suffering, aridity, weariness, even infidelity and sin.*

—Brother Lawrence of the Resurrection

Every question I ask as a spiritual director is a variation of one
of the following: "Can you clarify that for me?" or "Where
do you sense God's presence in that?" I ask the first question
to help my directees ponder the second one. According to
Brother Lawrence of the Resurrection, only the second question
really matters.

In a conversation with Joseph de Beaufort, Brother
Lawrence shared a story. On a winter morning, he was looking
at a tree that had lost all its leaves. As he pondered the tree, he
realized that the leaves would soon reappear, bloom flowers,
and yield fruit.

Now, if I had been Brother Lawrence's spiritual director, I would have asked, "Did you have any sense of God's presence as you looked at the tree?"

Based on Joseph de Beaufort's account, Brother Lawrence might have responded, "Yeah, I had an incredible sense of God's providence."

"Can you describe it?" I might ask.

"Well," the virtual Brother Lawrence might say, "it's *more intense than fire*. It's *more luminous than the sun in a clear sky*."

I would rest in silence as he waited for the Holy Spirit to prompt him.

"You know," he'd continue, "*I don't know what*. All I can really say is that *God is incomprehensible.*"

Brother Lawrence didn't run off and join a religious order right away. That came six years later, after he had fought in the Thirty Years' War, during which he was wounded, tried to live as a hermit, and served as a personal valet. In 1640, he joined the Order of Discalced Carmelites in Paris as a lay brother. Lawrence worked as a cook and a sandal maker and was even responsible for buying wine for his community. More important, many sought his instruction for practicing the presence of God.

It's simple, really: "The practice of the presence of God is an application of our mind to God, or a remembrance of God present, that can be brought about by either the imagination or the understanding." It's the habit of constantly bringing the mind back into God's presence so that "all our actions, without exception, become a brief conversation with God."

This practice is not mere piety—it is the very life and nourishment of the soul. It is a habit that leads one to find God.

Awareness and Practice

You bestow on him blessings forever;
*   you make him glad with the joy of your presence.*

—Psalm 21:6

Each Person of the Holy Trinity practices the perfect presence of each other Person. God the Father is perfectly aware of God the Son and God the Holy Spirit. Each Person is entirely and wholly attuned to the other two. Because their practice is perfect and constant, they are constantly united to one another. When you practice the presence of God, you live the Mystery of the Holy Trinity because you are participating in *their* practice.

Stop. Put this book down. Turn your mind to God and offer thanks, adoration, and praise. Use a simple phrase that will gently turn your awareness to God. (Brother Lawrence suggests "My God, I am completely yours" or "God of love, I love you with all my heart.")

Do this frequently, no matter what you may be doing, even during prayer or other spiritual activities. This practice will intensify your faith, strengthen your hope, and draw you closer into God's unfathomable love.

47

Inscape

Gerard Manley Hopkins

1844–1889

There is one notable dead tree . . . the inscape markedly holding its most simple and beautiful oneness up from the ground through a graceful swerve below (I think) the spring of the branches up to the tops of the timber.

—Gerard Manley Hopkins

Gerard Manley Hopkins had a genius idea that he called *inscape*. Basically, *inscape* means that God does not use a Xerox machine in the act of creation. No two things are ever the same, yet they all do the same thing, each in its own way: all things reveal the glory of God.

The Jesuit poet's genius wasn't in the idea itself: the thirteenth-century Franciscan philosopher John Duns Scotus coined a term he called *haecceitas*—"thisness"—to describe the property that was responsible for individual identity. *Thisness* explains that *this* thing is not *that* thing.

Rather, Hopkins's genius was in how he explained this concept in the poem "As Kingfishers Catch Fire":

As kingfishers catch fire, dragonflies draw flame;
As tumbled over rim in roundy wells
Stones ring; like each tucked string tells, each hung bell's
Bow swung finds tongue to fling out broad its name;
Each mortal thing does one thing and the same:
Deals out that being indoors each one dwells;
Selves—goes itself; *myself* it speaks and spells,
Crying *What I do is me: for that I came.*

I say more: the just man justices;
Keeps grace: that keeps all his goings graces;
Acts in God's eye what in God's eye he is—
Christ—for Christ plays in ten thousand places,
Lovely in limbs, and lovely in eyes not his
To the Father through the features of men's faces.

The kingfisher and dragonfly create a visual spectacle in flight, but the way a kingfisher "catches fire" is different from how a dragonfly "draws flame." Throwing a rock into a well, plucking on the string of a harp, or ringing a bell—each of these produces sounds, but each sound is distinct from the other (no one would confuse a rock dropped in a well with a note plucked on the string of a harp). The "inscape" or "thisness" of each of these things—its unique identity—is revealed through its actions, actions that ultimately reveal God. "Each mortal thing does one thing and the same"—namely, proclaim God's glory. Christ, after all, "plays in ten thousand places, / Lovely in limbs, and lovely in eyes not his."

As the "Just man justices"—that is, the inscape of a just person is that the person acts justly—the inscape that we all share is to find God, each in our own unique way.

Awareness and Practice

"I made your name known to them, and I will make it known,
so that the love with which you have loved me may be in them,
and I in them."

—John 17:26

God the Father, God the Son, and God the Holy Spirit each has a unique and distinct inscape. The inscape of God the Father is that of *parent*—provider, protector, and teacher. The inscape of the Son is that of *child*—vulnerable, innocent, and growing. The inscape of the Holy Spirit is that of *wisdom*—"pure, then peaceable, gentle, willing to yield, full of mercy and good fruits, without a trace of partiality or hypocrisy" (James 3:17).

Yet, since there is unity among the Three Persons of the Trinity, their inscapes must be one. Perhaps that unity can be seen in their harmony. Yes, the inscape of God the Father is that of a parent, but God acts as a parent in the way of a child—vulnerable, innocent, and growing—as well as with wisdom—pure, peaceable, full of mercy, etc. So, too, with the other Persons.

You can live the Mystery of the Trinity by living out your own *inscape*. How do your actions reveal your unique identity? How is your unique identity reflected in your actions? What does this identity tell you about God? What does your inscape tell others about God? How does it influence the way in which you find God? How does your inscape reflect the inscape of each Person in the Trinity?

48

Detachment

Meister Eckhart

1260–1327

He who seeks God while seeking other things will never find God. But if someone really seeks nothing other than God, he finds God—and never quite alone, for all that God can offer he finds together with God. If you seek God, and if you seek him for your own advantage and for your own beatitude, then in truth you are not looking for God at all.

—Meister Eckhart

My dad is a *huge* opera fan, and while most of my knowledge of opera is limited to the classic Bugs Bunny cartoon "Rabbit of Seville," I have gone to a few operas with him. My favorite is *Das Rheingold* by Richard Wagner, which opens with three water nymphs—the Rhinemaidens—singing at the bottom of the river Rhine. A dwarf named Alberich tries to woo them, and the Rhinemaidens reject his advances, humiliating him in the process.

After watching this opening scene for the first time, I thought that the river Rhine must be a weird place. And after reading some of the works of the great Dominican mystic

Meister Eckhart, I'm convinced that there was indeed something in the water.

Meister Eckhart's teaching rested on a concept he called *grund* in German, or "ground." In describing *grund*, Eckhart explained, "It is neither this nor that, and yet it is a something. . . . It is free of all names and devoid of all forms, entirely bare and free, as void and free as God is in himself. It is perfect unity and simplicity as God is unity and simplicity, so that in no way can one peer into it."

To understand God in unity and simplicity, Eckhart taught that one had to be perfectly detached from all things. But detachment is not a passive act—it is not the act of forgetting oneself to penetrate the mystery of God. (God being one in unity and simplicity, Eckhart would probably think that penetrating the mystery of God is an impossibility.) Rather, detachment is a process. It begins with "virginity" (freedom) and continues with "fertility" (being reborn in God the Father). Free of any attachments—that is, things that lead a person away from God—the detached person gives birth to Christ in the world. This gift is the work of the Holy Spirit, resulting in thanksgiving and praise.

"It is the plain truth," Eckhart explains, "that whatever you strive after other than God himself can never be so good as to not obstruct your way to the supreme truth." The detached person seeks God, who alone is perfectly good, supremely good, and the *only* good.

Everything else—no matter how good it may seem to be—is an obstruction.

Awareness and Practice

"As you, Father, are in me and I am in you, may they also be in us, so that the world may believe that you have sent me."

—John 17:21

The receptive heart of God the Son receives the gift of God the Spirit from God the Father. Each Person is perfectly free, and each gives thanks and praise for the other two. In their detachment, all three Persons dissolve into the unity of God.

Practice detachment in prayer by not seeking answers, favors, or consolations. Rather, pray for no other reason than to simply be with God.

Practice detachment in your possessions. Think not in terms of ownership but in terms of use. How does a thing help you grow closer to God?

Finally, practice detachment from intention. Eckhart explains, "A poor man wills nothing, knows nothing, and has nothing." Whatever your plans, aims, or goals, remember that they are not God's plans, they are yours.

49

Divine Love

Mechthild of Magdeburg

c. 1207–c. 1282

True love praises God constantly;
Longing love give the pure heart sweet sorrow;
Seeking love belongs to itself alone;
Understanding love loves all in common;
Enlightened love is mingled with sadness;
Selfless love bears fruit without effort;
It functions so quietly
That the body knows nothing of it.

—Mechthild of Magdeburg

I remember going to a Foreigner concert, and when I heard them play "I Want to Know What Love Is," I asked myself a better question: "I want to know why I am at a Foreigner concert?" I would have preferred seeing AC/DC.

But the question posed in that Foreigner song is still a good one to ponder. What is love? More important, what is *divine* love?

Mechthild of Magdeburg explains the answer in *The Flowing Light of the Godhead*, which she wrote sometime around

1270, after joining the Cistercian convent in the town of Hefta. In it, she describes mystical union as the love shared between Christ and the soul, between bridegroom and bride. This love has five characteristics.

First, divine love demands righteousness. "If," Mechthild explains, "I see my friend act wrongly toward my enemy and God's enemy, then I blame my friend and lovingly help my enemy." In other words, love supersedes loyalty toward one's "tribe."

Second, love demands compassion. When we see a person in need, we help them, and such help is based on the need of the person, not on our affection toward them. As Mechthild explains, "If I see my friend and my enemy in equal need, I shall help both equally." Such compassion encourages those we comfort to share their needs with God so that God may help them.

Third, love demands fidelity. We remain true to our friends no matter what, and in times when fidelity is tested, we are obliged to reconcile with one another.

Fourth, love demands silence when we are aggravated, bothered, or otherwise upset. Harsh words come from prideful and angry hearts, Mechthild warns, and they should not be spoken. In such silence, she assures us, we can find God's endless grace.

Fifth, love demands humility. We need to be honest about ourselves, our motivations, our desires, and our fears. We can rejoice in knowing that God sees directly into our heart, and we have nothing to be ashamed of. Shame, after all, leads us to hide from God and others.

For Mechthild, finding God was nothing more than falling in love, for love lifts us to the transcendence of God. And it is through love that the transcendent God becomes immanent. In other words, love allows us to know that which is unknowable.

Awareness and Practice

Beloved, let us love one another, because love is from God; everyone who loves is born of God and knows God. Whoever does not love does not know God, for God is love.

—1 John 4:7–8

"I was created in love," says the Soul in *The Flowing Light of the Godhead*, "therefore nothing can express or liberate my nobleness save Love alone." When we practice divine love—when we are righteous, compassionate, faithful, silent, and humble—we best reflect the action of each Person of the Holy Trinity. (After all, this is how God loves us.) Only then will we truly see in ourselves the image and likeness of God.

Bring to mind someone you know. Do you love that person with divine love? Is your love for that person independent of the group that person belongs to? Do you show that person compassion, even when that person seems not to deserve it? Do you choose to remain silent when you are tempted to judge and condemn that person? Do you approach that person with humility, understanding that like you, they are a mystery in and of themselves?

Repeat this exercise with others, with yourself, and finally, with God.

50

Paradox

Richard Rohr

b. 1943

*Each one of us must learn to live with paradox, or we cannot live
peacefully or happily even a single day of our lives. In fact, we must
even learn to love paradox, or we will never be wise, forgiving, or
possessing the patience of good relationships.*

—Richard Rohr

Suppose there is a town that has only one barber, and this barber has a rule that he will shave every man in the town who doesn't shave himself. But what about the barber? Does he shave himself? If you say no, then he is someone who doesn't shave himself, and by his own rule, he must shave himself (he shaves every man who can't shave himself, and he is one of those men). If you say yes, then he is shaving someone who can shave himself. Therefore, by his own rule, he must not shave himself.

You might think that the barber has a stupid rule. However, it's a good example of Russell's Paradox, named after the British mathematician and Nobel laureate Bertrand Russell (1872–1970). This paradox unraveled the attempt by another mathematician named Gottlob Frege (1848–1925) to develop a foundation for all of mathematics using symbolic logic.

Paradoxes like this are not always problems for mathematicians because they lead to new developments in the field. For example, Russell's Paradox led to what's called a "theory of types" that imposed a hierarchy upon mathematical objects—numbers, sets of numbers, sets of sets of numbers, etc.—and helped establish a philosophical foundation for mathematics.

Paradoxes aren't obstacles to finding God either, because to find God, you have to learn how to hold the contradictions in life. To find God, you have to learn how to use a nondualistic mind as opposed to a dualistic one.

The Franciscan friar Richard Rohr explains the difference between the two. The dualistic mind is binary. It divides things into *this* or *that*. It compares and differentiates. That can be useful (computers, which are *really* useful, communicate in binary code using zeros and ones). The problem with this kind of thinking is that it is not helpful in dealing with mystery; it would rather classify things as one thing or another, as right or wrong.

Mystery requires a nondualistic mind. "The nondual mind," teaches Rohr, "is open to everything. It is capable of listening to the other, to the body, to all the senses. It begins with a radical yes to each moment." The nondual mind learns that you don't need to divide things. Instead, it seeks to hold everything—the good *and* the bad, the light *and* the darkness, the zeros *and* the ones—in a loving gaze where everything belongs.

Paradoxes can help us break free of the dualistic mind and see a bigger picture. Paradoxes, in other words, help us grow beyond finding God in *this* thing or *that* thing so that we can find God in *all* things.

Awareness and Practice

If you think that you are wise in this age, you should become fools so that you may become wise.

—1 Corinthians 3:18

"The doctrine of the Trinity," writes Richard Rohr, "was made to order to defeat the dualistic mind and invite us into nondual, holistic consciousness." The dualistic mind wants to think of God the Father, God the Son, and God the Holy Spirit as three distinct individuals. It gets tripped up over the fact that they are one.

The nondual doesn't analyze the Trinity. It doesn't try to divide the Three Persons, nor does it try to force them together. Rather, it knows how to be present to the paradox that is the Trinity.

Living the Mystery of the Trinity requires comfort with paradox. Pay attention to the contradictions in your life. When you notice that you are using dualistic thinking to categorize objects, people, or ideas—phrases like "it's either this or that" or "that's true and that's false" are dead giveaways—stop and take a breath. Look at them with detachment: they are neither *this* nor *that*. They just *are*. Pay close attention to any wisdom that emerges from such a restful gaze.

51

Forgetfulness

An Anonymous Mystic

Fourteenth Century

A man may know completely and ponder thoroughly every created thing and its works, yes, and God's works too, but not God himself. Thought cannot comprehend God. And so, I prefer to abandon all I can know, choosing rather to love him whom I cannot know.
—*The Cloud of Unknowing*

Perhaps one of the greatest books about Christian mysticism is *The Cloud of Unknowing*, which was written by an anonymous English author sometime in the late fourteenth century. I imagined having a conversation with the author as I read it.

In this conversation, I proudly explain my ideas about how to find God in all things: "Instead of trying to find God, we should simply try to live with God."

"Stop that," the author implores me. "Don't take this the wrong way, but your mind is too small to comprehend God."

I don't know if there is any other way to take it. I am offended.

"Look," the author continues, trying to heal my wounded pride, "it's impossible for humans to think about God; he is beyond human intellect. If you want to find God, then you need to be comfortable stumbling around in the darkness."

I raise my voice, challenging the author. "How can I be at home in the darkness when Christ is the light that chases it away?" Gotcha. There is no darkness. I win! Yay me!

"You don't understand—"

"Obviously," I interrupt. "You've made that abundantly clear."

"It's a figure of speech," the author continues, ignoring my interruption. "By 'darkness' I mean the absence of knowledge: either you don't know, you don't understand, or you can't remember."

I roll my eyes. The author is nuts.

"This unknowing is what separates human beings from God," he continues. "It's like a cloud between us. That's what makes being human so hard."

"So I find God by not finding God? That makes no sense."

"That's because you're thinking about it! Look." The author sighs. "It's like this: Just as there is a cloud of unknowing between you and God, you have to put a cloud of forgetting between you and everything else."

"Come again?"

"Don't *think* about the words you will use to praise God. Don't *think* about the mysteries of God. Don't *think* about how you will help others praise God. That will just distract you by focusing on words, events, and actions rather than on the one and only thing you *should* be focusing on: God and God alone!"

"Then what am I supposed to do?" I give up.

"Nothing. Simply rest between the cloud of forgetting and the cloud of unknowing and allow your desire to love God grow."

I close my copy of *The Cloud of Unknowing*, ending this phantom dialogue. I'm more confused about finding God than ever before. Perhaps that's what progress looks like.

Awareness and Practice

I pray that you may have the power to comprehend, with all the saints, what is the breadth and length and height and depth, and to know the love of Christ that surpasses knowledge, so that you may be filled with all the fullness of God.

—Ephesians 3:18–19

The Most Holy Trinity, the central mystery of the Christian faith, lies hidden deep within the cloud of unknowing. No clever analogy can help us know or understand this mystery. "Only love," writes our anonymous fourteenth-century English author, "can touch God as he is in himself." So forget everything you know or think you know, and desire only love. For the more you love, the more you will desire to love, for love's desire is love itself.

Forget everything you think you know about God. Or rather, realize that everything you think you know about God is just a stab in the dark. Every time you formulate a conception of God, negate it by saying, "God is not that; God is more." Only then can you let God be God; only then will you be able to find God in all things.

Awareness

Ronald Rolheiser

b. 1947

We all have mystical experiences, though we aren't all mystics.
—Ronald Rolheiser

I've been asking myself a question lately: How will I know when I've found God? (Alternatively, how will I know God has found me?)

The popular Catholic writer, speaker, and retreat leader Fr. Ron Rolheiser offers a possible answer: when I have what can be called a *mystical moment.*

We have mystical moments, he explains, when "we know ourselves and our world with clarity, even if just for a second. That can involve something extraordinary, like a vision or apparition, but normally it doesn't." A mystical moment is extraordinary not because we have angelic visitors but "because of its unique lucidity and clarity, because for that moment, we are extraordinarily centered."

My friend and mentor Tom McGrath shares an example of a mystical moment:

When I was a kid, probably about 9 or 10 years old, I took to climbing a big old mulberry tree in our backyard. In summer I could hide among its branches unbeknownst to those going about their lives below. And I would simply enjoy the fresh breeze and just be.

One morning in particular stands out for me. As I propped my back against the main trunk of the tree, nestled between two branches, my mind slowed and my attention drifted. In a kind of hyper-awareness, I could feel the light breeze and smell the warmth of the sun on the earth below and with an unusual clarity I spotted a single ant crawling along a nearby branch. The rest of the world slipped away. I was focused on that ant and I felt the world open up in a new way, like when I went for my vision test that year and the doctor flipped the lens in place that removed all the blur and revealed a crisper, clearer world than I'd become used to. Time stood still. I felt no lack, no desire. I was one with the tree that was supporting me, the breeze that was refreshing me, the sun whose light and warmth I was immersed in, the murmur of sounds reassuring me, the life of this ant, which was connected to my life and mine to its life. The tree was the cosmos, and God was present, sustaining it all.

I didn't have these words to articulate what I was experiencing at that early age, but I did have the experience which remains both out of time and vividly real. It wasn't the only time I felt a mystical connection to a life greater than mine up in that tree—and many places elsewhere over the years. And it may not have been the first. But it felt so complete and "really real" that I have come to rely on its truth whenever doubt enters my heart. It tells me, "God is near. This life is God's life poured out for me, for us—including the ants. All is right with the world."

"We all have experiences like these," says Rolheiser, and I agree. The important thing is not how many of these moments we have or how intense those moments can be; rather, the only thing that matters is our awareness of those mystical moments. That awareness leads us to God.

Awareness and Practice

Open my eyes, so that I may behold
wondrous things out of your law.

—Psalm 119:18

We live the Mystery of the Holy Trinity in the mystical moments when we experience the clarity of God's perfect love and the harmony it brings us—not just within ourselves but with all things. While our mystical moments are fleeting and infrequent, for each Person of the Trinity, such experiences are not momentary but permanent and constant: God the Son has perfect clarity of how much he is loved by God the Father and

God the Holy Spirit. The same is true for God the Father and God the Holy Spirit. That is why there is perfect harmony among all Three Persons.

Spend time reflecting on when you may have had mystical moments of clarity, peace, connectedness. You may not have the words to articulate what you felt or experienced, and that's fine. Simply name the moment and give thanks. The more you recall and reflect on those moments, the more you will be open to recognizing them as you go about your days.

Epilogue

Ignatius of Loyola

1491–1556

They should practice the seeking of God's presence in all things, in their conversations, their walks, in all that they see, taste, hear, understand, in all their actions, since his Divine Majesty is truly in all things.

—Ignatius of Loyola

The idea of finding God in all things is not that radical to me. As a Secular Franciscan, my tradition affirms that all created things point to the Creator. I can find God in a bird, a rock, or a tree because those things were created by—and are therefore loved by—God.

So when I first heard someone summarize Ignatian spirituality—that is, the spirituality based on St. Ignatius of Loyola and the *Spiritual Exercises*—I wasn't all that impressed. "Franciscans have been doing that for centuries," I thought. "Welcome to the club."

I suspect that Ignatius was talking about something different, something deeper. He was sharing his realization that we find God not so much in the things we encounter; we find

God in *the act of encounter itself.* I don't find God in this thing or that thing. I find God in *the encounter* with things. That is, *God* is a verb meaning "to encounter with love." That's how we find God in all things.

God made the universe a place of encounter. All of creation is a temple where we can worship. No wonder Ignatius put so much emphasis on freedom: Only someone who is truly detached—someone who doesn't prefer health over sickness, wealth over poverty, but only seeks God's will—is someone who can find God in all things.

I think that's the lesson that Ignatius and the mystics want me to learn: the universe is a sacred encounter. Time for me to ponder that for a while.

Why don't you ponder this mystery with me?

Stop what you are doing. Look around you. What is the encounter you are living in this very moment? Is it a conversation? A breeze across your face? A strong emotion? How do you experience love at this exact moment?

Ask God, "Where are you? For I long to see your face."

Acknowledgments

My heartfelt thanks to everyone who walked with me as I worked on this book.

Thank you, Susan Taylor, Gaston Philipps, and Vinita Hampton Wright, for your skillful editing. You helped me find the words that escaped me.

Thank you, Rosemary Lane, for listening to me as I struggled to understand my own thoughts.

Thank you, Tom McGrath, for sharing your mystical moments with me.

Thank you, Porter Moser, for teaching me how to trust in my writing process.

Thank you, Joe Paprocki, for ensuring that my words remain rooted in the Catholic faith.

Thank you, Loyola Press, for giving me the opportunity to share my words.

Thank you, Sisters of Saint Joseph of the Third Order of Saint Francis **and the entire Franciscan family**, for your inspiration.

Thank you, dear reader, for inviting me into your own spiritual journey.

Thank you, all people of good will, for your wisdom and compassion that continue to reveal to me God in all things.

And most of all, thank you, Cathy Burnham, for everything. Why you married me will always remain a mystery.

About the Author

Bob Burnham is a Secular Franciscan, a spiritual director, catechist, and the author of *Little Lessons from the Saints: 52 Simple and Surprising Ways to See the Saint in You*. He lives in the Chicago suburbs with his wife and two Siberian huskies.